Gabriele Redden

OVEN-BAKED

VEGETARIAN DISHES

PHOTOGRAPHY

Heinz-Josef Beckers

Cover Photo:

Michael Brauner

Translation from the German:

Elizabeth D. Crawford

BARRON'S

TABLE OF CONTENTS

Enjoying Vegetarian Cooking

With their wealth of shapes, sizes, and colors, vegetables are the most irresistible food we have. The possibilities for preparing them and combining them are simply endless. Oven-baked dishes are especially appealing because they have something so wonderfully nostalgic about them.

Gratins or casseroles that come out of the oven with a golden crust on top magically create a homey atmosphere around the table and delight family and guests alike.

Dishes from the oven are ideal for entertaining: not only do they look appetizing, they smell and taste even better. Even if they might take a little time to prepare, they will cook on their own while you mingle with your guests.

Why Is a Vegetarian Diet So Healthy?
As a rule, vegetables are low in fat and calories but rich in minerals and vitamins—or what nutritionists call "nutrient-dense."

Be Careful About Variety and Freshness
Make sure you plan your menus with plenty of variety and use the freshest possible foods. It is vital to choose representatives from each food group. Include daily products, bread and grains, rice, noodles, and fresh vegetables and fruits in season. According to recent findings, the color of fruits and vegetables is important: the more intense it is, the more vitamins the produce contains. For fats, choose seed and olive oils when possible; use clarified butter, butter, and margarine moderately, and avoid saturated fats like lard and solid shortening.

What Should You Drink?

Mineral water is always correct; choose the still or the sparkling kind as you prefer. Juices containing vitamin C are important because vitamin C dramatically improves the body's assimilation of iron from plant foods. Coffee and tea are less suitable as a drink with food because they bind iron, making it more difficult for the body to utilize it.

What About Wine?

But of course you need not refuse a glass of wine—it's especially good with oven-baked dishes. Follow your personal taste when choosing wine. Many red wines go well with the vegetable gratins, but so does a light Italian Verdicchio or a German or California Riesling. The only tricky choice is which wine to serve with tomato dishes, which are very flavor-intensive. A sturdy Chianti or Rioja is a good choice, but you might prefer another. Simply trust your palate.

A Brief Guide to Metric Measurements

1 teaspoon sugar = 5 g
1 tablespoon sugar = 15 g
1 teaspoon flour = 2 g
1 tablespoon flour = 6 g
1 teaspoon oil = 5 g
1 tablespoon oil = 8 g
1 tablespoon butter = 15 g
1 teaspoon salt = 3 g
1 tablespoon salt = 10 g
1 tablespoon = 3 teaspoon
a pinch = about ⅛ teaspoon

It's what's
INSIDE
that counts

Subtly Filled

Succulent "fruit" vegetables like egg-plants, tomatoes, and peppers are perfect for stuffing. Various fats and oils provide their respective nuances.

About Fats and Oils

Without fat many dishes would only taste half as good; it provides the golden crust on casseroles and gratins, it makes dough workable, and, not least, it is responsible for the transport of the important vitamins A, D, and E.

Butter is available in different versions, which differ in taste and degree of acidity. Butter must by U.S. law be at least 80 percent milk fat. The remaining 20 percent consists of water and milk solids.

• Unsalted butter is usually labeled as such and contains absolutely no salt. Unsalted butter is preferred by many for everyday eating and baking. Because it contains no salt (which acts as a preservative), it is more perishable than salted butter and therefore stored in the freezer section of some supermarkets.

• Whipped butter has had air beaten into it, thereby increasing volume and creating a softer, more spreadable consistency when cold. It comes in salted and unsalted forms.

• Light or reduced-calorie butter has water, skim milk, and gelatin. It shouldn't be substituted for regular butter or margarine in frying and baking.

Storing butter:
Butter is sensitive to light, warmth, and odors. Because butter absorbs flavor like a sponge, it should be wrapped airtight for storage. In a sealed container in the refrigerator, it keeps for up to 3 weeks.

Clarified butter can be safely used for 6 to 8 weeks after it has been opened. To make it, melt a stick or more of butter and pour off the clear butterfat, discarding the milky solids. The pure fat is very good for broiling, deep frying, baking, and general cooking.

Margarine tolerates high temperatures, so it is particularly suitable for cooking, frying, and baking.

Sunflower oil comes from the seeds of the sunflower. Because of its high content of vitamin E and other ingredients, it is considered a particularly high-value oil. Its mild taste and its sunny yellow color make it one of the most popular oils for cold and hot cookery. In dark glass bottles or in a dark, cool place it will keep for up to 10 months.

Olive oil is high in healthful monounsaturated fats and is prized for its outstanding fruity flavor. There are three grades of olive oil available: "Extra virgin" and "virgin" are cold-pressed, and "olive oil" is a mixture of cold-pressed and refined oil. Kept tightly closed and stored at temperatures no higher than 64°F (15°C), olive oil keeps for up to 18 months.

Canola oil has been discovered to be lower in saturated fat content (about 6 percent) than any other oil. It also contains more cholesterol-balancing monounsaturated fat than any other oil except olive oil. Canola oil is suitable both for cooking and for salad dressings.

Ovenware

Soufflé dishes
are round and deep. They come in various sizes between 4¾ and 8¾ inches (12–22 cm) and are made of glass, heat-resistant porcelain, stoneware, or pottery.

Casserole dishes
are round, oval, or rectangular, of medium depth, and have a diameter of about 9¾ × 6 inches (25 × 15 cm) to 11¾ × 15¾ inches (30 × 40 cm). They are made of heat-resistant porcelain, stoneware, pottery, glass, enamel, or cast iron.

Au gratin dishes
are shallow and round or oval. They come in widths of 4 to 11¾ inches (10–30 cm), in stoneware, pottery, or heat-resistant porcelain.

Springforms
can of course be used for baking casseroles, etc.

Baking sheets
are also suitable for some oven dishes, as are pizza pans.

Tomatoes with Feta Cheese

Tomatoes with Feta Cheese

1 bunch oregano

1 garlic clove

14 oz feta cheese

1 tablespoon crème fraîche
or sour cream

black pepper

8 tomatoes

olive oil

*Preparation time:
about 20 minutes*

Tomatoes with Gorgonzola

8 tomatoes

1 bunch basil

1 scallion

3½ oz (100 g) gorgonzola

1 tablespoon bread crumbs

1 teaspoon green
peppercorns

1 egg

salt

butter

*Preparation time:
about 35 minutes*

Tomatoes with Feta Cheese

Pictured • Can be used for a first course

• Wash the oregano, shake dry, and chop. Peel the garlic and press it. Mash the feta cheese with a fork and mix with the oregano, garlic, crème fraîche, and pepper.

• Wash the tomatoes and dry them. Cut off the tops and set aside. Hollow out the tomatoes with a teaspoon (reserve the pulp) and fill with the cheese mixture. Replace the tops.

• Grease a baking dish with olive oil and place the reserved tomato pulp in the dish. Set the tomatoes on top. Broil 3 to 5 minutes or until the cheese is flecked golden brown. Makes 4 servings.

Tip

If you don't have a broiler, the tomatoes can be baked in an oven preheated to 450°F (250°C) (center, convection 445°F [230°C]) for about 8 minutes.

PER SERVING:	325 CALORIES
NUTRITIONAL INFORMATION	

Fat (32% calories from fat)	16	g
Protein	19	g
Carbohydrate	18	g
Cholesterol	49	mg
Sodium	25	mg

Tomatoes with Gorgonzola Filling

Easy • Piquant

• Preheat the oven to 350°F (180°C). Grease a shallow casserole. Wash the tomatoes and dry them. Cut off the tops and set aside. Carefully hollow out the tomatoes and place the removed pulp in the casserole.

• Wash the basil and pat it dry. Finely chop the leaves. Wash the scallion, trim, pat it dry, and chop. Crumble the gorgonzola into a dish and mix it with the bread crumbs, peppercorns, and egg. Season the mixture with salt to taste.

• Stuff the tomatoes with the cheese filling and replace the tops. Arrange the tomatoes in the casserole and bake (center, convection 320°F [160°C]) for about 20 minutes. Makes 4 servings.

PER SERVING:	178 CALORIES
NUTRITIONAL INFORMATION	

Fat (64% calories from fat)	13	g
Protein	10	g
Carbohydrate	6	g
Cholesterol	155	mg
Sodium	14	mg

Potatoes with Porcini Filling

Inexpensive • Pictured

• Soak the porcini in lukewarm water for about 2 hours. Wash the potatoes thoroughly and dry them. Bake them at 350°F (180°C) (convection 320°F [160°C]) for about 1 hour. Remove from oven and let cool. Halve the potatoes and hollow them out, leaving a shell about ¼ inch (1 cm) wide. Reserve the potato pulp.

• Preheat the oven to 475°F (250°C). Oil a baking sheet. Mix the sour cream with the potato pulp and season with salt and pepper. Rinse the porcini well, pat them dry, and chop them fine. Wash the chives, shake them dry, and chop them fine. Fold them into the potato mixture with the mushrooms.

• Fill the potato shells with the mixture, arrange on the baking sheet, and bake (convection 440°F [230°C]) for about 10 minutes. Makes about 4 servings.

PER SERVING:	98 CALORIES
NUTRITIONAL INFORMATION	
Fat (29% calories from fat) 3	g
Protein 2	g
Carbohydrate 16	g
Cholesterol .10	mg
Sodium 5	mg

Peppers with Rice

Exotic • Easy to make

• Bring the broth to a boil. Peel onion and dice very fine. Heat clarified butter and sauté onion until almost tender. Add the coriander, cumin, cardamom, cloves, and cinnamon sticks. Add pine nuts and raisins and sauté over moderate heat for about 3 minutes. Add rice and fry briefly, then pour in vegetable broth and cook for about 20 minutes. Remove the cinnamon sticks and cloves.

• Meanwhile, bring a large quantity of water to boil. Preheat oven to 350°F (180°C). Oil a baking dish. Wash the peppers, cut off tops, and remove seeds. Blanch peppers in boiling water for about 3 minutes. Arrange them in the dish and fill with rice mixture. Replace the tops. Distribute the rest of the filling around them and drizzle with ¼ cup (2 fl oz/60 ml) water. Bake the peppers (convection 320°F [160°C]) for about 15 minutes. Makes 4 servings.

PER SERVING:	453 CALORIES
NUTRITIONAL INFORMATION	
Fat (32% calories from fat) 16	g
Protein 11	g
Carbohydrate 68	g
Cholesterol .14	mg
Sodium 878	mg

Potatoes with Porcini Filling

¾ oz (20 g) dried porcini mushrooms (cèpes)

4 large baking potatoes

¼ cup (2 oz/60 ml) sour cream or crème fraîche

salt

pepper

1 bunch chives

oil for the baking sheet

Preparation time: about 2 hours and 20 minutes (of which 1¾ hours are soaking, baking, and cooling time)

Peppers with Rice

2 cups (16 fl oz/500 ml)) vegetable broth

1 onion

2 tablespoons clarified butter

¼ teaspoon ground coriander

¼ teaspoon ground cumin

¼ teaspoon ground cardamom

5 whole cloves

4 cinnamon sticks

2 ounces (60 g) pine nuts

¼ cup (1 oz/30 g) golden raisins

7 oz (200 g) rice

4 each small red and green bell peppers

oil for the dish

Preparation time: about 50 minutes

For the sauce:

4 red bell peppers

1 onion

2 cloves garlic

2 tablespoons olive oil

2 teaspoons dried thyme

4 tomatoes

1 tablespoon white wine
vinegar

1¼ cups (10 fl oz/300 ml)
vegetable stock (page 59)
or broth

salt

pepper

For the lasagne rolls:

8 lasagne noodles

salt

3½ oz (100 g) button
mushrooms

2 tablespoons olive oil

2 tablespoons pine nuts

½ bunch sage

14 oz (400 g) ricotta cheese

1 egg

salt

pepper

2 tablespoons freshly grated
Parmesan cheese

oil for the baking dish

Preparation time:
about 1 hour and
20 minutes

Lasagne Rolls with Pepper Sauce

A hit with children • For company

• For the sauce, broil the peppers for about 15 minutes, turning them several times, until the skin blisters. Let cool under a damp towel. Peel, halve, remove seeds and white pith, and dice.

• Peel and mince the onion and garlic. Heat the oil and sauté the onion and garlic in it along with the thyme. Remove the stem bases from the tomatoes and blanch the fruit. Halve crosswise, squeeze out the seeds, and dice. Add the tomatoes to the onion mixture with the vinegar and vegetable stock. Add the peppers and puree all with a hand blender or food processor. Simmer the sauce until somewhat reduced and season with salt and pepper.

• Boil the lasagne in plenty of salted water for about 10 minutes. Drain the lasagne and spread it out on dish towels. Preheat the oven to 350°F (180°C). Grease a wide baking dish.

• Trim the mushrooms, wipe them off thoroughly, and dice them fine. Heat the oil in a skillet, and cook the mushrooms in it over medium heat for about 5 minutes, until the liquid is cooked away. Let cool.

• Roast the pine nuts in a nonstick pan. Wash the sage, shake it dry, and chop the leaves. Mix the ricotta with the mushrooms, pine nuts, sage, and egg. Season with salt and pepper.

• Spread some pepper sauce on the bottom of the baking dish. Place a spoonful of ricotta mixture on the center of each lasagne piece. Roll up the lasagne and place in the dish, seam side down. Pour the remaining sauce over the rolls. Sprinkle with Parmesan and cover with aluminum foil. Bake the lasagne rolls (convection 320°F [160°C]) for about 20 minutes. Makes 4 servings.

PER SERVING:	654 CALORIES
NUTRITIONAL INFORMATION	
Fat (42% calories from fat) . . . . .31 g	
Protein . . . . .29 g	
Carbohydrate .67 g	
Cholesterol . . . . .208 mg	
Sodium . . . . .623 mg	

Savory Stuffed Mushrooms

For a buffet • Pictured

• Thoroughly wipe off the mushrooms, but if possible, do not wash them. Twist out the stems and chop them fine.

• Peel and mince the shallots and garlic. Heat 2 tablespoons butter and sauté both until nearly tender. Add the mushroom stems and salt. Pour in the white wine and cook down over moderate heat. Transfer the mixture to a bowl.

• Preheat the oven to 350°F (180°C). Oil a shallow baking dish. Wash the parsley and thyme, pat them dry, and pick off the leaves. Chop the parsley. Add the herbs, cheese, bread crumbs, and egg to the shallot mixture and knead together. Add salt and pepper and fill the mushroom caps with the mixture.

• Arrange the mushrooms in the baking dish. Melt the rest of the butter and brush over the mushrooms. Bake (convection 320°F [160°C]) for about 15 minutes. Makes 4 servings.

PER SERVING:	262 CALORIES	
NUTRITIONAL INFORMATION		
Fat (66% calories from fat)	19	g
Protein	10	g
Carbohydrate	12	g
Cholesterol	110	mg
Sodium	8	mg

Herbed Tomatoes

Can be used as a first course • Easy

• Preheat the oven to 400°F (200°C). Grease a baking dish.

• Wash the tomatoes, halve, and carefully hollow out with a teaspoon. Place the tomato pulp in the dish. Wash the basil, parsley, oregano, and thyme, and pat dry. Chop the herb leaves and mix with the bread crumbs.

• Peel the garlic and put through a press into the herbs. Wash the scallions, pat them dry, cut them into thin rings, and add to the herbs. Whisk the egg yolk and olive oil together and fold into the herb mixture. Season to taste with salt and pepper and fill the tomato halves with the mixture.

• Arrange the tomatoes in the baking dish and bake (convection 350°F [180°C]) for about 15 minutes. Makes 4 servings.

PER SERVING:	155 CALORIES	
NUTRITIONAL INFORMATION		
Fat (26% calories from fat)	5	g
Protein	5	g
Carbohydrate	26	g
Cholesterol	80	mg
Sodium	30	mg

Savory Stuffed Mushrooms

12 large mushrooms

2 shallots

2 cloves garlic

4 tablespoons butter

salt

3 tablespoons dry white wine (or vegetable broth)

½ bunch parsley

½ bunch thyme

2¾ oz (75 g) hard cheese (e.g., Parmesan or Gruyère), freshly grated

1½ oz (40 g) bread crumbs

1 large egg

pepper

oil for the baking dish

Preparation time: about 30 minutes

Herbed Tomatoes

8 medium tomatoes

2 bunches basil

1 stalk each parsley, oregano, and thyme

1¾ oz (50 g) bread crumbs

4 cloves garlic

4 scallions

1 egg yolk

1 tablespoon olive oil

salt

pepper

oil for the baking dish

Preparation time: about 30 minutes

17

4 medium zucchini

4 tablespoons butter

salt

2 shallots

9 oz (250 g) button
mushrooms

⅔ cup (5 oz/150 ml) dry
white wine

½ bunch parsley

½ bunch tarragon

2 egg yolks

1 tablespoon whole-wheat
bread crumbs

pepper

⅓ cup (3½ fl oz/100 ml)
vegetable broth

1 tablespoon sour cream or
crème fraîche

butter for the baking dish

*Preparation time:
about 1¼ hours*

Zucchini with Mushroom Stuffing and Wine Sauce

Easy • Can be prepared ahead of time

• Preheat the oven to 350°F (180°C). Grease a large, shallow baking dish. Wash the zucchini, dry, and trim it. Halve the squash and scoop out the insides with a spoon, leaving a ⅛-inch (5-mm) shell. Coarsely chop the removed zucchini.

• Heat 1 tablespoon butter and sear the zucchini pulp for about 5 minutes over high heat. Season to taste with salt and let as much liquid as possible cook off.

• Peel and finely dice the shallots. Heat 2 tablespoons butter and sauté the shallots in it until transparent. Add the mushrooms and salt and sauté for several minutes. Add 3 tablespoons white wine and cook over moderate heat, stirring, until it has evaporated.

• Wash the parsley and tarragon, pat them dry, and chop the leaves. In a bowl, mix the fried zucchini pulp, mushrooms, 1 egg yolk, herbs, and bread crumbs. Season to taste with salt and pepper. Spoon the filling into the zucchini halves.

• Arrange the stuffed zucchini in the baking dish. Dot with the remaining butter and pour the rest of the wine and the vegetable broth over them. Bake the zucchini (convection 320°F [160°C]) for about 20 minutes.

• Remove the zucchini from the baking dish and keep warm. Whisk the wine and broth with the sour cream and the remaining egg yolk and heat, stirring, until the sauce is slightly thickened, but do not let it boil. Serve the sauce with the stuffed zucchini. Makes 4 servings.

PER SERVING:	207 CALORIES
NUTRITIONAL INFORMATION	

Fat (61% calories from fat) 13	g
Protein 6	g
Carbohydrate 13	g
Cholesterol 184	mg
Sodium 186	mg

Cheese-Stuffed Eggplant

Easy • For company

• Wash the eggplants and halve them lengthwise. Using a teaspoon, hollow them out, leaving a ⅛-inch (5-mm) shell. Wash the carrot, scallion, and zucchini, pat them dry, and trim, peeling the carrot. Finely chop the carrot and zucchini; cut the scallion into thin rings.

• Preheat the oven to 475°F (250°C). Grease a baking dish. Heat the clarified butter and olive oil and cook the vegetables in it without browning, then add 2 tablespoons water and cook over low heat for 15 minutes. Let cool, then puree. Mix with egg yolk and bread crumbs and season with salt, pepper, and paprika. Fill the eggplants with the mixture and place them in the baking dish.

• Crumble the Roquefort, mix with cream cheese and cream, and spread over the eggplants. Cover with foil and bake (convection 445°F [230°C]) for 10 minutes. Remove the foil and bake about 5 minutes longer. Makes 4 servings.

PER SERVING:	235 CALORIES	
NUTRITIONAL INFORMATION		
Fat (65% calories from fat) 17		g
Protein 7		g
Carbohydrate 14		g
Cholesterol 120		mg
Sodium 237		mg

Stuffed Kohlrabi

Pictured • Can be used as a first course

• Wash and peel the kohlrabi. Bring the vegetable stock to boil and cook the kohlrabi in it for about 15 minutes. Remove and let cool, then halve them crosswise.

• Meanwhile, heat the oven to 350°F (180°C). Grease a baking dish. Clean the mushrooms and slice them. Heat the butter and sauté the mushrooms in it for about 2 minutes. Wash the spinach leaves and let them wilt in ½ cup (4 fl oz/125 ml) boiling water. Place 2 spinach leaves and several mushroom slices on each of the 8 kohlrabi halves. Cover with the remaining halves and arrange in the baking dish. Bake (convection 320°F [160°C]) for about 10 minutes.

• Peel the garlic and put it through a press. Mix with the mustard, grated cheese, white wine, and cream. Season with salt and pepper.

• Spread the cheese mixture over the kohlrabi and brown them in the oven for about 4 minutes. Makes 4 servings.

PER SERVING:	198 CALORIES	
NUTRITIONAL INFORMATION		
Fat (55% calories from fat) 12		g
Protein 13		g
Carbohydrate 10		g
Cholesterol .28		mg
Sodium 248		mg

Cheese-Stuffed Eggplant

2 large eggplants

1 carrot

1 scallion

1 small zucchini

1 tablespoon clarified butter

1 tablespoon olive oil

1 egg yolk

3 tablespoons bread crumbs

salt • pepper

1 teaspoon sweet paprika

1¾ oz (50 g) Roquefort cheese

3½ oz (100 g) cream cheese

1 tablespoon cream

grease for the baking dish

Preparation time: about 55 minutes

Stuffed Kohlrabi

8 small, tender kohlrabi

⅓ cup (3½ fl oz/100 ml) vegetable broth

4 large mushrooms

1 tablespoon butter

16 spinach leaves

1 clove garlic

1 tablespoon hot mustard

1¾ oz (50 g) each pecorino and Parmesan cheese, freshly grated

3 tablespoons white wine (or vegetable broth)

3 tablespoons cream

salt • pepper

butter for the baking dish

Preparation time: about 55 minutes

Kept in Shape

Baked in a Flaky Pastry Crust

No one can resist vegetables when they take the form of savory pies, pastries, and soufflés.

Vitamins—Catalysts in the Body

Vitamins A, D, E, and K are fat-soluble, which means that they are stored in body fat.

• Vitamin A is needed for healthy eyes, skin, hair, fingernails, and mucous membranes, and it supports the immune system. It is found in green and red vegetables (especially carrots and spinach), and in cheese and eggs.

• Vitamin D is required for the body to properly utilize calcium. If you get plenty of sunlight, the body produces the amount it needs.

• Vitamin E protects the body from free radicals, which destroy hormones and enzymes. In addition, it helps limit the carcinogenic effects of many environmental pollutants. It is found in salsify, celery root, avocados, and peppers.

• Vitamin K is responsible for blood clotting. It is found in yogurt, egg yolk, canola oil, and leafy green vegetables.

The B vitamins are water soluble. The body cannot store them, so they must be continually replenished.

They provide for properly functioning metabolic processes and a strong nervous system. B vitamins are especially concentrated in grains, nuts, yeast, green vegetables, soybeans, eggs, and milk products. Meat is a good source of vitamin B_{12}, but milk and cheese are good substitutes for vegetarians.

Vitamin C is also water soluble. It repairs, develops, and strengthens the connective tissue and promotes the development of bone. A sufficient quantity of vitamin C protects against bleeding gums, cataracts, varicose veins, and hemorrhoids. It provides for increased development of the immune cells that fight back in case of a viral or bacterial infection. And, along with vitamins A and E, it is one of the important vitamins for immune function. Peppers, broccoli, Brussels sprouts and other cabbages, fennel, strawberries, citrus fruit, and kiwis are important sources of vitamin C.

Minerals

are the building blocks for bones, blood plasma, teeth, and hair.

• **Iron** is found primarily in meat and is responsible for the development of red blood cells. For vegetarians, lentils, whole-grain products, nuts and seeds, spinach, dried fruits, egg yolks, brewer's yeast, and wheat germ are good alternative sources of iron.

• **Calcium** is necessary for bones, teeth, muscles, and nerves. It is abundant in milk and milk products.

• **Zinc** is needed for the body's growth and healing processes. It is present in wheat germ, cheese, brewer's yeast, dried figs, nuts and peas, mangoes, and spinach.

• **Magnesium** provides for healthy nerve and muscle function, among other things. It occurs in wheat germ and unpolished rice, but especially in green vegetables, kohlrabi, and corn.

• **Iodine** is essential for thyroid gland function. The tiny quantities that we need are contained in lettuce, mushrooms, and iodized table salt.

• **Potassium** plays a part in *metabolism*, the process by which organisms change food into energy and new tissue. For example, potassium helps enzymes speed up some chemical reactions in the liver and the muscles. Such reactions produce a carbohydrate called *glycogen*, which regulates the level of sugar in the blood and helps provide energy for muscles. Potassium, together with sodium, also contributes to the normal flow of water between the body fluids and cells. Fruits, especially bananas, and vegetables, such as potatoes, are good sources of potassium.

Fiber

regulates digestion and binds pollutants, moving them out of the body. Legumes, cabbage, root and leaf vegetables, whole-grain products, and fruit are among the foods that are especially plentiful in fiber.

Energy-producing Protein

is essential, along with carbohydrates. Vegetarian cuisine finds its sources of protein in legumes, rolled oats, eggs, milk, yogurt, cheese, and tofu. These foods also contain many important minerals and B vitamins.

The Stars of Vegetarian Cuisine

These foods contain the most vital nutrients per weight:

<u>*Vegetables*</u>
Broccoli, kale, fennel, Brussels sprouts, spinach, peppers, carrots, kohlrabi

<u>*Fruit*</u>
Black currants, red currants, strawberries, kiwis, papayas, raspberries, mangoes, blueberries

<u>*Grains*</u>
Wheat sprouts, rolled oats, rye, barley, unpolished rice, millet, unripe spelt

<u>*Nuts/Legumes*</u>
Peanuts, sunflower seeds, hazelnuts, cashews, Brazil nuts, white beans, lentils, chickpeas

Feta Cheese-Herb Soufflé

For the experienced • Decorative

• Preheat the oven to 400°F (200°C). Grease an 8-inch (20-cm) soufflé dish. Dice the feta cheese into a bowl. Add the eggs and ricotta and blend until creamy with a hand mixer, sprinkling in the flour while beating.

• Wash the herbs, pat dry, and finely chop the leaves. Peel the garlic and put through a press into the cheese mixture. Add the herbs, salt, and pepper and mix all together once more.

• Spread the mixture in the dish. Bake the soufflé (convection 350°F [180°C]) about 25 minutes. Turn off the oven and let the soufflé rest for about 5 more minutes in the oven, then serve immediately. A tossed salad goes well with this. Makes 4 servings.

PER SERVING:	370 CALORIES	
NUTRITIONAL INFORMATION		
Fat (52% calories from fat) 22	g
Protein 32	g
Carbohydrate 12	g
Cholesterol .482	mg
Sodium 5	mg

Zucchini Soufflé

Classic • Pictured

• Wash and dry the zucchini. Grate it and pour off the liquid.

• Preheat the oven to 375°F (190°C). Heat the milk. Melt 3 tablespoons of the butter in a saucepan over moderate heat. Whisk in the flour, then gradually whisk in the hot milk. Mix in salt, pepper, and nutmeg and stir until the sauce thickens. Remove it from the heat. Stir in the rest of the butter.

• Separate the eggs. Butter a soufflé dish well. When the milk mixture has cooled somewhat, stir in the egg yolks one at a time. Pat the grated zucchini dry and fold in along with the cheese. Beat the egg whites stiff and fold them into the mixture.

• Spoon the zucchini-cheese mixture into the soufflé dish. Sprinkle with cheese and bake (convection 338°F [170°C]) for about 35 minutes, until the soufflé has risen high and the top is nice and brown. Serve immediately. Makes 4 servings.

PER SERVING:	501 CALORIES	
NUTRITIONAL INFORMATION		
Fat (70% calories from fat) 35	g
Protein 21	g
Carbohydrate 13	g
Cholesterol .390	mg
Sodium 3	mg

Pepper-Tomato-Zucchini Turnovers

Somewhat time consuming • Also good at room temperature

• For the dough, heap the flour on a work surface and make a well in the center. Add the yeast, honey, salt, olive oil, milk, and ⅔ cup (5 oz/150 ml) lukewarm water to the well and knead by hand or with a dough hook to form a smooth dough.

• Let the dough rise, covered, in a warm place for 1 hour or until doubled in bulk.

• Meanwhile, for the filling, peel the onion and garlic and chop finely. Wash and dry the pepper and zucchini; halve, clean, and dice finely. Blanch the tomatoes, peel them, halve them crosswise, squeeze out the seeds, and dice them, discarding the stem bases.

• Heat the olive oil in a skillet. Sauté the onion and garlic until transparent, then over higher heat for about 3 minutes, stirring, until they take on color. Add the pepper and zucchini and sauté together for about 3 minutes while stirring, adding the paprika near the end. Add the tomatoes and let the vegetables cook down over higher heat, stirring, for about 10 minutes. Allow to cool somewhat.

• Heat the oven to 350°F (180°C). Grease a large baking sheet. Punch the dough down and roll it out on a floured work surface to form a rectangle about 14 × 19 inches (35 × 47.5 cm). Cut it into 12 squares, about 4¾ inches (12 cm) on a side.

• Thoroughly mix the combined vegetables in a bowl with the cheese and egg and season to taste with salt and pepper. Put about 2 tablespoons filling on each dough square, fold the dough over into a rectangle, and lightly press around the edges to seal. Brush with beaten egg yolk. Arrange the turnovers on an oiled baking sheet and bake (convection 320°F [160°C]) until golden brown, about 20 minutes. Makes 4 servings.

PER SERVING:	773 CALORIES	
NUTRITIONAL INFORMATION		
Fat (35% calories from fat) 29	g
Protein 31	g
Carbohydrate 90	g
Cholesterol .252	mg
Sodium 14	mg

For the dough:
4 cups (18 oz/500 g) whole-wheat flour
1 envelope instant dry yeast
1 teaspoon honey
1½ teaspoon salt
3 tablespoons olive oil
⅔ cup (5 fl oz/150 ml) lukewarm milk

For the filling:
1 onion
8 cloves garlic
1 small green bell pepper
10 oz (300 g) zucchini
18 oz (500 g) tomatoes
3 tablespoons olive oil
2 teaspoons sweet paprika
7 oz (200 g) freshly grated pecorino cheese
1 egg
salt
pepper
flour for the work surface
olive oil for the pan
1 egg yolk for glaze

Preparation time:
about 2½ hours (of which about 20 minutes is baking time)

29

For the ricotta dough leaves:

7 oz (200 g) ricotta or cottage cheese

1¾ cups (7 oz/200 g) all-purpose flour

¼ teaspoon salt

7 oz (200 g) cold butter

For the filling:

2 onions

1 clove garlic

14 oz (400 g) mushrooms

3½ oz (100 g) morels (or additional mushrooms)

8 stalks parsley or 4 stalks lovage

2 tablespoons butter

2 oz (50 g) almonds, chopped

1 tablespoon cream

1 egg

salt

pepper

flour for the work surface

1 egg yolk for glaze

Preparation time: about 1¾ hours (of which about 20 minutes per pan is baking time)

Turnovers with Mushroom-Almond Filling

For company • Somewhat time consuming

• For the dough, allow the ricotta or cottage cheese to drain in a sieve. Heap the flour on a work surface, add the salt, and place the butter on it in small pieces. Chop in with a knife. Then quickly work the mixture into a smooth dough, gradually kneading in the cheese. Form a ball, wrap it in plastic wrap, and place it in the freezer for about 40 minutes.

• For the filling, peel onions and garlic and chop finely. Trim the mushrooms, clean them well, and slice them. Thoroughly rinse the morels, pat them dry, and dice them. Wash the parsley, shake it dry, and chop the leaves.

• Heat the butter in a large skillet. Fry the onions and garlic in it until they are transparent. Add the mushrooms, morels, and parsley and cook over moderate heat for about 10 minutes, then over higher heat for about 3 minutes to boil off some of the mushroom liquid, stirring constantly. Let cool slightly, then mix in the almonds, cream, and egg. Season with salt and pepper.

• Preheat the oven to 350°F (180°C). Grease a baking sheet. Halve the dough and leave one half in the refrigerator. Dust the work area and rolling pin with flour and roll out the dough about ⅛ inch (3 mm) thick. Cut into squares about 4¾ inches (12 cm) on a side. Put about 2 tablespoons of filling in the center of each and fold over each square on the diagonal. Arrange turnovers on an ungreased baking sheet, brush with egg yolk, and bake (convection 320°F [160°C]) for about 20 minutes or until golden brown. Makes 4 servings.

Variation:

Leek-Cheese Turnovers

For the filling, sauté 18 oz (500 g) sliced leeks in 1 tablespoon of butter for about 4 minutes. Mash 4½ oz (125 g) each of Roquefort and Camembert cheese with a fork and work into a paste with 2 eggs. Mix with 2 tablespoons of ground green peppercorns, salt, and the leek. Assemble turnovers and bake as described.

PER SERVING:	827 CALORIES
NUTRITIONAL INFORMATION	
Fat (65% calories from fat) 60	g
Protein 22	g
Carbohydrate 51	g
Cholesterol 369	mg
Sodium 16	mg

For the dough:
4 cups (18 oz/500 g) whole-wheat flour, or more as needed
1 envelope instant yeast
½ teaspoon salt
2 tablespoons olive oil

For the topping:
6 small artichokes
2 small eggplants
2 red bell peppers
4 large cloves garlic
½ teaspoon chili powder
7 tablespoons olive oil
salt
5 oz (150 g) feta cheese
3½ oz (100 g) mozzarella cheese
1 bunch basil
pepper
olive oil for the pan
flour for the work surface

Resting time:
about 2½ hours

Preparation time:
about 1½ hours (of which about 20 minutes per pan is baking time)

Pizza with Artichokes and Feta Cheese

A classic • Children love it

• For the dough, make a sponge by mixing 1 cup (3½ oz/100g) flour, the yeast, and ½ cup (3½ fl oz/100 ml) lukewarm water. Let it rise in a warm place for about 30 minutes.

• Heap the remaining flour on a work surface and make a well in the center. Add the salt, olive oil, and the yeast sponge and knead together.

• Gradually work in another ½ cup (3½ fl oz/100 ml) water and knead into a smooth, elastic dough. Let it rise, covered, in a warm place for about 2 hours.

• Preheat the oven to 400°F (200°C). Grease a baking sheet. For the topping, wash the artichokes, eggplants, and peppers and pat them dry. Thinly slice the eggplants and halve the peppers; remove the centers with the seeds. Arrange them on the baking sheet with the garlic. Stir the chili powder into the olive oil and use part of it to brush onto the eggplant.

• Bake the vegetables (convection 350°F [180°C]) for about 20 minutes, turning the eggplant from time to time and brushing with more oil.

• Meanwhile, bring a large pot of salted water to boil. Cut the leaf tips and the stems from the artichokes and boil the artichokes for about 20 minutes.

• Raise the oven temperature to 475°F (250°C). Peel the peppers and the garlic; cut the peppers into matchstick-size pieces. Mash the garlic with a fork. Quarter the artichokes.

• Divide the pizza dough into 4 equal parts. On a floured work surface, roll out each to a circle about 8 inch (20 cm) in diameter. Put 2 pizzas on each of 2 baking sheets. Spread each with the remaining chili oil and the garlic. Distribute the artichokes, eggplant, and peppers on the dough. Crumble feta cheese over the pizzas and top with slices of the mozzarella. Wash the basil, shake it, chop the leaves, and sprinkle them over the pizzas. Drizzle with a little olive oil and season with salt and pepper. Bake at 475°F (250°C) (convection 450°F [230°C]) for about 20 minutes. Serve hot. Makes 4 servings.

PER SERVING:	774 CALORIES
NUTRITIONAL INFORMATION	
Fat (36% calories from fat) 31	g
Protein 34	g
Carbohydrate 87	g
Cholesterol .14	mg
Sodium 1	mg

Three-Cheese Calzones

Can easily be prepared ahead • Somewhat time consuming

• For the dough, make a sponge by mixing 1 cup (3½ oz/100 g) flour, the yeast, and ½ cup (3½ fl oz/100 ml) lukewarm water. Let it rise in a warm place for about 30 minutes.

• Heap the remaining flour on a work surface and make a well in the center. Add the salt, olive oil, and the yeast sponge and knead together.

• Gradually add ½ cup (3½ fl oz/100 ml) lukewarm water and knead into a smooth, elastic dough. Place the dough in a bowl, cover with a cloth, and let rise in a warm place for about 2 hours. It should double in bulk.

• Preheat the oven to 475°F (250°C). For the filling, place the ricotta in a bowl and mix with the egg. Add the Parmesan. Cut the mozzarella into small dice and mix in.

• Cut the stem bases out of the tomatoes. Blanch the tomatoes, halve them crosswise, seed, and chop finely. Wash the basil, shake it dry, pick off the leaves, and chop them. Mix the tomatoes and basil with the cheese and season with pepper.

• Oil the baking sheet. Knead the dough on a floured work surface for several minutes. Divide into 4 equal pieces and roll each into a circle about ⅛ inch (3 mm) thick.

• Distribute the filling on half of each piece of dough, leaving a border at the edge. Dampen the edges, fold the dough over, and press the edges together. Place two calzones on each baking sheet and let rest in a warm place for about 15 minutes, then bake them (convection 450°F [230°C]) for about 20 minutes. Makes 4 servings.

For the dough:
4 cups (18 oz/500 g) whole-wheat flour, or more as needed
1 envelope instant yeast
½ teaspoon salt
2 tablespoons olive oil

For the filling:
9 oz (250 g) ricotta cheese
1 egg
2⅔ oz (75 g) Parmesan cheese, freshly grated
7 oz (200 g) mozzarella cheese
3 large tomatoes
1 bunch basil
black pepper
flour for the work surface
olive oil for the baking sheet

Preparation time:
about 3½ hours (of which 2¾ hours is resting time and about 20 minutes is baking time)

PER SERVING:	780 CALORIES	
NUTRITIONAL INFORMATION		
Fat (36% calories from fat) 31	g
Protein 43	g
Carbohydrate 81	g
Cholesterol .194	mg
Sodium 59	mg

5 frozen phyllo sheets
(10½ oz [300 g])

1¾ oz (750 g) spinach

2 leeks

2 cloves garlic

2 sprigs each rosemary,
thyme, and marjoram

3 tablespoons butter

2 teaspoons green
peppercorns

grated rind of 1 small orange

salt

7 oz (200 g) feta cheese

7 oz (200 g) ricotta cheese

2 eggs

2 oz (50 g) pine nuts

flour for the work surface

olive oil for the baking dish

1 egg for glazing

Preparation time:
1–1¼ hours (of which
40–50 minutes is baking
time)

Spinach-Cheese Pie
For company • Can be used as an appetizer

• Spread out the phyllo leaves and let them thaw. Preheat the oven to 400°F (200°C). Grease a 12½-inch (32-cm) pie plate. Pick over the spinach and wash it. Cook for 3 minutes over high heat in the water clinging to the leaves, then let cool and squeeze out as much moisture as possible. Chop the leaves coarsely. Trim the leeks, wash, and slice them into rings. Peel and mince the garlic. Wash the herbs, shake them dry, and chop.

• Melt the butter in a skillet and sauté the leek in it for 2 to 3 minutes without browning. Add the garlic, herbs, peppercorns, orange peel, and salt and cook for another 3 minutes. In a bowl mix the spinach, cheeses, and eggs. Season to taste with salt.

• Lay 3 phyllo sheets on top of one another on a floured work surface and roll out to a circle 13½ inches (34 cm) in diameter. Place in the pie plate and sprinkle with the pine nuts. Add the filling and spread it out evenly.

• Brush the edges of the filled phyllo sheets with egg. Place 2 phyllo sheets on top of each other and roll out to a circle 12½ inches (32 cm) in diameter. Place over the filling and press on

edges to seal. Trim off any overhanging dough. Brush the entire top with egg yolk and bake the pie (convection 350°F [180°C]) for 40 to 50 minutes. Makes 4 to 6 servings.

Variation:
Ricotta-Basil Tart

Roll out 2 sheets of phyllo together to make a pastry base 10¼ inch (26 cm) in diameter. Place in an oiled baking dish. Fill with dried beans or pie weights and bake the pastry in a preheated 400°F (200°C) (convection 350°F [180°C]) oven for about 10 minutes. Remove the beans or weights. Mix 1¾ oz (50 g) chopped basil, 2 tablespoons olive oil, 12 oz (350 g) ricotta, and 3 tablespoons grated Parmesan with pepper briefly in the food processor. Stir in 3 eggs and 5 tablespoons cream. Finely chop 1½ oz (30 g) dried tomatoes and mix with 12 black olives, chopped. Spread the mixture on the dough and bake as described.

PER SERVING:	537 CALORIES
NUTRITIONAL INFORMATION	
Fat (67% calories from fat) . . . . 41 g
Protein . . . . 22 g
Carbohydrate . . . . 23 g
Cholesterol .355 mg
Sodium . . . . 104 mg

For the dough:
1¾ cups (7 oz/200 g) whole-wheat flour
1 egg yolk
½ teaspoon honey
½ teaspoon salt
7 tablespoons ice-cold butter
5 tablespoons ice water

For the filling:
3 bunches chives
4 eggs
scant ½ cup (3½ oz/100 g) cream
⅔ cup (5⅓ oz/150 g) crème fraîche or sour cream
2 oz (60 g) Gruyère cheese, freshly grated
freshly grated nutmeg
salt
pepper
flour for the work surface
grease for the pan

Preparation time: about 1½ hours

Chive Quiche
Suitable for an appetizer • For company

• For the dough, heap the flour on a work surface, and make a well in the center. Add the egg yolk, honey, and salt to the well. Place pieces of the butter on top and cut in with a pastry blender. Gradually knead the ice water into the dough. Wrap the dough in plastic and place in the freezer for about 30 minutes. Meanwhile, preheat the oven to 350°F (180°C).

• Dust the work surface and a rolling pin with flour and roll the dough out to form a 12-inch (30-cm) circle. Grease a 10-inch (26-cm) springform and lay the dough in it, forming a rim about ¾ inch (2 cm) high all around. Fill the pastry shell with dried beans or pie weights and bake (convection 320°F [160°C]) for 10 minutes. Remove the beans or weights; leave the oven on.

• For the filling, wash the chives, shake them dry, and slice them into thin rings. Beat the eggs and stir them with the cream and crème fraîche until smooth. Add the cheese and the chives and season to taste with nutmeg, salt, and pepper. Pour the filling into the pastry shell. Bake the quiche in the center of the oven for about 20 minutes. Makes 6 servings.

Variation:
Broccoli-Camembert Quiche
For the filling, cook 10½ oz (330 g) broccoli florets for 8 minutes and spread them over the pastry in the pan. Beat 4 eggs and 1 cup (8 fl oz/250 ml) cream with salt, pepper, and nutmeg and pour over the broccoli. Distribute 5⅓ oz (150 g) ripe Camembert in slices over the top in a rosette design. Bake the quiche as above.

PER SERVING:	410 CALORIES	
NUTRITIONAL INFORMATION		
Fat (71% calories from fat) 32		g
Protein 8		g
Carbohydrate 22		g
Cholesterol .136		mg
Sodium 0		mg

UNDER
THE
TOPPING

Delicious Gratins

Topped with sauce, cheese, or beaten egg whites, seasoned with fresh herbs, and run under the broiler, vegetables make an elegant dish indeed.

The Most Important Herbs in Brief

What would vegetable cooking be without herbs? They turn cooking into an adventure. They are wonderfully easy to grow at home in the garden or in pots on the balcony. Here are my must-haves for the dishes in this book.

Basil

makes us think of Mediterranean cooking, but it comes from tropical India. With its wonderful aroma and flavor it underscores the quintessential flavor of tomatoes, peppers, zucchini, and many other vegetables.

A tip for gardeners:
Basil is not winter hardy; it can be sown in a semishady spot after the beginning of May. Eight weeks later you can start seasoning dishes with your very own basil.

Dill

was already known in ancient Egypt for its calming effects. It is good to use for preserving cucumbers and other vegetables, in herb marinades, and in cottage cheese. But dill also tastes good in egg dishes and on potatoes and root vegetables.

A tip for gardeners:
It's best to sow the seeds in April in a sunny corner of your garden. About 8 weeks later you can clip the first bunch. It self-sows abundantly for a new crop the following year.

Marjoram

comes from North Africa and was already a favorite seasoning in ancient times. Its hearty flavor gives a special spice to fried potatoes and other fried dishes.

A tip for gardeners:
Plant in May in a protected corner of the garden; sometimes it even survives the winter. You can start harvesting in July. If picked before it flowers, margoram can also be dried.

Oregano

grows wild in central Europe, Asia Minor, North Africa, and all the way up to the Himalayas. It is associated above all with pasta and pizza.

A tip for gardeners:
A perennial, oregano is the more robust brother of marjoram. It can be harvested in July if sown in May in alkaline soil. It is good dried, with no loss of flavor, if picked before flowering.

Parsley

is undoubtedly the best-known herb, used in cuisines all over the world.

A tip for gardeners:
If you sow parsley in May, you can start harvesting it in about 8 weeks and continue well into October. Parsley is an annual and should not be dried; it loses its flavor.

Rosemary,

which is dedicated to Aphrodite, is a purely Mediterranean shrub. Monks brought it to northern Europe and used it as a medicinal herb and to ward off bad spirits. In the kitchen it is good on potatoes, eggplant, tomatoes, and zucchini.

A tip for gardeners:
In cold-winter climates, rosemary is best grown in pots so it can be moved to a warm place in winter, for it is very frost-sensitive.

Chives

are familiar for their onionlike flavor; they are native to Central Asia. They do not tolerate cooking, so they are added to hot dishes shortly before serving.

A tip for gardeners:
Chives can be sown starting in April. After 8 weeks you can begin cutting them.

Thyme

is found around the Mediterranean, especially on rocky coasts. It is prized as a seasoning for tomatoes, eggplant, zucchini, and legumes.

A tip for gardeners:
Thyme only thrives in sunny, protected spots. If you sow it in May, you will have the fresh herb for your pasta dishes all summer long.

Subtle Herb Sauces

Both go with many gratins, casseroles, and quiches. Let your taste decide.

Salsa Verde

(Makes 1 cup/ 250 ml)
Puree 3 shallots, 3 bunches parsley, 2 bunches basil, 2 garlic cloves, 3 tablespoons capers, the peel and juice of 1½ lemons, scant ¾ cup (6 fl oz/175 ml) olive oil, salt, and pepper in the food processor.

The sauce keeps in an airtight jar in the refrigerator for 1 week. It should be at room temperature for serving.

Mint-Yogurt Sauce

(Makes 1½ cups (12 fl oz/350 ml)
Stir together 1¼ cups (10 oz/300 g) whole-milk yogurt, 1 tablespoon olive oil, ½ teaspoon lemon juice, salt, and pepper. Mix in 2 bunches mint, chopped, and 1 clove garlic, pressed. Chill for 1 hour before serving.

This sauce does not keep well.

Endive-Tomato Gratin

Very easy • Inexpensive

• Preheat the oven to 400°F (200°C). Bring a pot of salted water to boil. Trim and wash the endive, pat it dry, and halve it lengthwise. Blanch for about 2 minutes. Wash the tomatoes and slice them crosswise, removing the stem bases. Grease a large, shallow casserole. Arrange the endive halves and the tomatoes alternately in the casserole. Brush the vegetables with olive oil and season with salt and pepper.

• Wash the scallions and herbs; chop them. Peel and mince the garlic. Sprinkle all over the vegetables. Drizzle with the remaining olive oil. Sprinkle Parmesan and bread crumbs over the top and dot with the butter.

• Bake the gratin (convection 350°F [180°C]) until the topping is golden, about 15 minutes. Makes 4 servings.

PER SERVING:	251 CALORIES	
NUTRITIONAL INFORMATION		
Fat (53% calories from fat)	15	g
Protein	8	g
Carbohydrate	23	g
Cholesterol	.28	mg
Sodium	.40	mg

Fennel with Parmesan Topping

Pictured • Subtly complex

• Bring a pot of salted water to boil. Trim fennel bulbs, wash, and cut in half. Cook for about 10 minutes until al dente, then drain.

• Meanwhile, peel and mince garlic. Remove stem bases from tomatoes, skin them, halve horizontally, and chop coarsely, discarding the seeds. Heat 1 tablespoon butter and the olive oil in a pot. Add garlic, tomatoes, salt, and pepper and let them cook over medium heat for about 15 minutes, stirring as needed. Meanwhile, preheat oven to 400°F (200°C). Wash herbs, shake them dry, and chop. Stir them into the sauce.

• Grease a gratin dish, put in the fennel bulbs, and pour the tomato sauce over them. Sprinkle bread crumbs, Parmesan, and lemon peel on top; dot with remaining butter. Bake (convection 350°F [180°C]) about 15 minutes or until the topping is golden. Makes 4 servings.

PER SERVING:	339 CALORIES	
NUTRITIONAL INFORMATION		
Fat (33% calories from fat)	20	g
Protein	64	g
Carbohydrate	24	g
Cholesterol	.38	mg
Sodium	.17	mg

Endive-Tomato Gratin

salt

4 large endives

4 medium tomatoes

2 tablespoons olive oil

pepper

2 scallions

2 sprigs each oregano, basil, and thyme

2 cloves garlic

1¾ oz (50 g) Parmesan cheese, freshly grated

3 tablespoons bread crumbs

2½ tablespoons butter

olive oil for the baking dish

Preparation time: about 30 minutes

Fennel with Parmesan Topping

salt

4 bulbs fennel

2 cloves garlic

1 lb (16 oz/750 g) tomatoes

4 tablespoons butter

2 tablespoons olive oil

pepper

½ bunch each basil, oregano, and thyme

1¾ oz (50 g) whole-wheat bread crumbs

1¾ oz (50 g) Parmesan cheese, freshly grated

grated peel of 1 small lemon

butter for the baking dish

Preparation time: about 50 minutes

1½ lb (700 g) eggplant

6 tablespoons olive oil

1 clove garlic

2 shallots

10 oz (300 g) tomatoes

1 bunch parsley

½ bunch basil

½ bunch oregano

½ bunch thyme

½ black olives

salt

black pepper

14 oz (400 g) mozzarella cheese

2 oz (60 g) Parmesan cheese, freshly grated

oil for the baking dish

*Preparation time:
about 45 minutes*

Eggplant-Tomato Gratin

Easy to make • Can be prepared in advance

• Preheat the oven to 350°F (180°C). Wash the eggplant, pat dry, peel, and cut into slices about ¼ inch (6 mm) thick. Brush a baking sheet with 1 tablespoon olive oil, arrange the eggplant slices on it, and drizzle them with 1 tablespoon olive oil. Bake them (convection 320°F [160°C]) for 15 minutes. Do not turn off the oven.

• Meanwhile, peel and finely chop the garlic and shallots. Remove the stem bases from the tomatoes. Blanch the tomatoes in boiling water and skin them. Cut the tomatoes into small pieces, discarding the seeds. Wash the herbs, pat them dry, and chop them finely.

• Heat the remaining olive oil in a pot and sauté the garlic and shallots in it. Add the tomatoes and simmer about 5 minutes. Stir in the herbs.

• Pit the olives, chop them coarsely, and add them to the sauce. Season to taste with salt and pepper.

• Brush a baking dish with 1 tablespoon oil. Remove the eggplant slices from the baking sheet and lay them upside down in the baking dish. Cover them with the tomato sauce. Slice the mozzarella and lay it over the eggplants. Sprinkle the gratin with Parmesan and bake (convection 320°F [160°C]) for 20 minutes. Makes 4 servings.

Variation:

Instead of eggplant, try zucchini or thin slices of trimmed fennel. Proceed the same way as for eggplant. This dish can be frozen.

PER SERVING:	476 CALORIES
NUTRITIONAL INFORMATION	

Fat (63% calories from fat) 34   g
Protein 28   g
Carbohydrate 16   g
Cholesterol 8   mg
Sodium 131   mg

Beans au Gratin

Hearty • Can be prepared ahead of time

• Peel and finely dice the onion. Cut the stem bases out of the tomatoes. Blanch the tomatoes, peel them, halve them crosswise, and dice, removing the seeds. Heat the olive oil and braise the onion and tomato in it for about 5 minutes. Add the drained red and white beans.

• Wash the savory, shake it dry, and chop it. Add to the beans with the bay leaf and the stock and simmer for about 20 minutes. Season with salt and pepper.

• Meanwhile, preheat the oven to 400°F (200°C). Grease a gratin dish and spread the bean mixture in it. Mix the Parmesan and bread crumbs and sprinkle over the beans. Melt the butter and drizzle it over the top. Brown the gratin in the oven (convection 350°F [180°C]) for about 20 minutes. Makes 4 servings.

PER SERVING:	675 CALORIES
NUTRITIONAL INFORMATION	
Fat (31% calories from fat) 16	g
Protein 27	g
Carbohydrate 51	g
Cholesterol 30	mg
Sodium .264	mg

Pasta Gratin

Pictured • Decorative

• Pick over the spinach and cook it in a little boiling water just until it wilts. Let it cool, squeeze out as much moisture as possible, and chop it.

• Preheat the oven to 475°F (250°C). Grease a baking dish. Bring a large pot of salted water to boil. Cook the pasta in it until al dente, then drain.

• Meanwhile, peel and mince garlic. Blanch tomato; skin and dice it, discarding stem bases and seeds. Wash basil, shake it dry, and cut the leaflets into fine strips.

• Heat the butter and sauté the garlic in it. Swish the spinach through it and remove. Briefly sauté tomatoes and basil without browning, and season with salt and pepper.

• Mix the pasta with olive oil and place in baking dish. Place the spinach in the middle and sprinkle with tomato. Dice cheese and sprinkle on top. Sprinkle pine nuts over it all and brown in the oven (convection 450°F [230°C]) for about 5 minutes. Makes 4 servings.

PER SERVING:	760 CALORIES
NUTRITIONAL INFORMATION	
Fat (34% calories from fat) 28	g
Protein 28	g
Carbohydrate 97	g
Cholesterol 18	mg
Sodium 45	mg

Beans au Gratin

1 onion

4 small ripe tomatoes

2 tablespoons olive oil

1 can each red and white beans (15 oz/425 g each)

2 sprigs savory

1 small bay leaf

2 tablespoons vegetable stock (page 77) or broth

salt • pepper

3½ oz (100 g) Parmesan cheese, freshly grated

1¾ oz (50 g) bread crumbs

3 tablespoons butter

butter for the baking dish

Preparation time: about 35 minutes

Pasta Gratin

9 oz (250 g) spinach

salt

1 lb (450 g) linguine

2 cloves garlic

1 large tomato

2 sprigs basil

2 tablespoons butter

pepper

2 tablespoons olive oil

3½ oz (100 g) Gorgonzola cheese

3½ oz (100 g) mozzarella cheese

4 tablespoons pine nuts

olive oil for the baking dishes

4 small gratin dishes

Preparation time: about 25 minutes

Asparagus Gratin

salt

1 teaspoon sugar

2 generous lbs (1 kg) asparagus

4 scallions

4 tablespoons butter

white pepper

2 oz (50 g) Gruyère cheese, freshly grated

4 tablespoons bread crumbs

butter for the baking dish

Preparation time: about 45 minutes

Oven-browned Green Beans

salt

2 generous lbs (1 kg) green beans

2 bunches scallions

7 oz (200 g) mushrooms

4 tablespoons butter

1 dried chili pepper

1 tablespoon all-purpose flour

1 cup (8 fl oz/250 ml) milk

freshly grated nutmeg

butter for the baking dish

Preparation time: about 50 minutes

Asparagus Gratin

Good for an appetizer • Fast

• Bring plenty of water to boil with 1 teaspoon salt and the sugar. Wash the asparagus and peel it; cut off the lower ends. Cook the asparagus in the water over medium heat for about 20 minutes.

• Meanwhile, preheat the oven to 475°F (250°C). Grease a shallow baking dish. Trim and wash the scallions and slice thinly. Heat half the butter and sauté the scallions in it until aromatic. Season with salt and pepper and remove from the heat.

• Lift the asparagus from the water, let it drain, and lay it in the baking dish. Sprinkle the cheese and scallions over it and sprinkle with the bread crumbs. Melt the remaining butter and drizzle it over the asparagus. Bake (convection 445°F [230°C]) for about 10 minutes. Makes 4 servings.

PER SERVING:	236 CALORIES
NUTRITIONAL INFORMATION	

Fat (64% calories from fat) 18	g
Protein 8	g
Carbohydrate 14	g
Cholesterol .38	mg
Sodium 7	mg

Oven-browned Green Beans

Pictured • Easy to make

• Bring a large pot of salted water to boil. Trim and wash beans. Cook them in salted water for about 10 minutes, then remove, rinse with cold water and let them drain. Preheat oven to 350°F (180°C).

• Meanwhile, trim and wash scallions and cut into thin rings. Clean the mushrooms and slice them paper-thin. Heat 3½ tablespoons butter in large skillet and sauté the onions and mushrooms in it for about 5 minutes. Mince the chili pepper and add.

• Melt remaining butter in a small saucepan. Brown the flour in it. Heat milk and whisk it in. Bring sauce to boil and season to taste with salt and pepper.

• Grease a shallow baking dish and lay the beans in it. Pour the sauce over. Sprinkle with the mushrooms and bake (convection 320°F [160°C]) for about 15 minutes. Makes 4 servings.

PER SERVING:	304 CALORIES
NUTRITIONAL INFORMATION	

Fat (49% calories from fat) 15	g
Protein 8	g
Carbohydrate 27	g
Cholesterol .41	mg
Sodium 25	mg

Polenta-Tomato Gratin

Special dish from the Piedmont • Easy

• For the polenta, combine 1 quart (1 l) of water and 1½ teaspoons salt in a large pot. Stir in the polenta gradually (so that it doesn't form lumps) and bring to boil, stirring constantly. Stir for 3 to 4 minutes over low heat, then cover, remove from heat, and let stand for about 10 minutes to thicken. Toast the pine nuts golden brown in a dry skillet. Wash the basil, pat it dry, and chop it. Stir it into the polenta with the pine nuts. Spread the mixture to a thickness of about ¼ inch (6 mm) on a damp dish towel and let it cool.

• Meanwhile, for the sauce, blanch and peel the tomatoes. Dice them, trimming away the stem bases. Wash the oregano and pull off the leaflets. Let the tomatoes, salt, and oregano cook down in a large pot over medium heat for about 30 minutes, stirring often.

• Preheat the oven to 400°F (200°C). Cut the polenta into diamond-shaped pieces about 3 × 1½ inches (7.5 × 3 cm). Cut the mozzarella into slices, the Gorgonzola into cubes.

• Butter a shallow casserole and cover the bottom with ⅔ of the tomato sauce. Alternate slices of polenta and mozzarella on the sauce, overlapping them. Sprinkle with the Gorgonzola, then drizzle with the remaining tomato sauce. Season with pepper and sprinkle with the Parmesan. Bake (convection 350°F [180°C]) for about 30 minutes. Makes 4 servings.

Variation:

For those who are not fond of polenta, semolina can be substituted; it has a somewhat blander flavor. The cooking times given also apply to semolina.

For the polenta:
1½ teaspoon salt
15 oz (225 g) precooked polenta
scant 1 oz (25 g) pine nuts
8 large basil leaves

For the sauce:
2 generous lb (1 kg) tomatoes
½ bunch oregano
1 teaspoon salt

For the topping:
7 oz (200 g) mozzarella cheese
generous 2½ oz (75 g) Gorgonzola cheese
pepper
generous 2½ oz (75 g) Parmesan cheese, freshly grated
butter for the baking dish

Preparation time: about 1½ hours

PER SERVING:	394 CALORIES
NUTRITIONAL INFORMATION	
Fat (53% calories from fat) . . . . 24 g	
Protein . . . . 24 g	
Carbohydrate . . . . 23 g	
Cholesterol .12 mg	
Sodium . . . . 21 mg	

Ingredients (sidebar)

Potato-Zucchini Gratin

salt
1¾ lb (750 g) firm-cooking potatoes
1¾ lb (750 g) zucchini
1 clove garlic
1 tablespoon butter
pepper
7 oz (200 g) Gouda cheese, coarsely grated
½ cup (4 fl oz/100 g) cream
freshly grated nutmeg

Preparation time: about 40 minutes

Mushroom Gratin

1¾ lb (750 g) firm-cooking potatoes
10 oz (300 g) mixed mushrooms
1 onion
1 clove garlic
½ bunch each thyme and marjoram
5 tablespoons butter
1 tablespoon tomato paste
3 tablespoons white wine or vegetable broth
3 tablespoons vegetable stock (page 77) or broth
salt • pepper
4 tablespoons milk
2 tablespoons cream
freshly grated nutmeg
1¾ oz (50 g) Emmentaler cheese, freshly grated
butter for the baking dish

Preparation time: about 1 hour and 20 minutes

Potato-Zucchini Gratin

Pictured • Good side dish

• Preheat the oven to 425°F (220°C). Bring a large pot of salted water to boil. Wash and peel the potatoes and slice them thinly. Cook in the boiling water for about 10 minutes. Wash the zucchini, dry, trim, and slice thin.

• Peel the garlic, press it, mix with a little butter, and use it to butter a baking dish. Alternate overlapping slices of potato and zucchini in the dish. Season with salt and pepper.

• Sprinkle the cheese over the top. Mix the cream and the nutmeg and pour it over. Bake the gratin (convection 400°F [200°C]) for about 15 minutes. Makes 4 servings.

Tip

Potato-zucchini gratin works very well as an accompaniment to grilled fish. The quantities given will then serve 6 people.

PER SERVING:	334 CALORIES	
NUTRITIONAL INFORMATION		
Fat (53% calories from fat) 20	g	
Protein 18	g	
Carbohydrate 22	g	
Cholesterol .55	mg	
Sodium 570	mg	

Mushroom Gratin

For company • Takes some time

• Wash and simmer potatoes in water to cover for 20 to 25 minutes or until tender.

• Trim and wipe mushrooms clean. Halve large ones lengthwise.

• Preheat oven to 425°F (220°C). Peel onion and garlic and chop finely. Wash the herbs, shake dry, and chop. Heat 2 tablespoons butter and sauté onion in it until transparent. Add mushrooms and sauté for about 3 minutes. Stir in tomato paste, half the herbs, and the garlic, and deglaze pan with wine. Pour in vegetable stock and simmer 3 minutes. Stir in remaining herbs and season with salt and pepper.

• Peel and mash potatoes. Stir in milk and cream; season to taste with salt, pepper, and nutmeg.

• Grease a shallow casserole and scatter the mushrooms in it. Distribute mashed potatoes on top. Sprinkle with cheese and dot with remaining butter. Bake (convection 400°F [200°C]) for about 18 minutes. Makes 4 servings.

PER SERVING:	292 CALORIES	
NUTRITIONAL INFORMATION		
Fat (37% calories from fat) 12	g	
Protein 9	g	
Carbohydrate 35	g	
Cholesterol .30	mg	
Sodium 123	mg	

LAYER
UPON
LAYER

Irresistible Casseroles

The basics of vegetarian cooking, as well as of casseroles and gratins, are of course the vegetables, which are available in inexhaustible variety. People whose meals consist mainly of vegetables, salads, legumes, grains, and potatoes consume less fat and animal protein, and, therefore take in more vitamins, minerals, and the all-important fiber. The most important vegetables are introduced here and on pages 76 and 77.

Vegetable Classifications

Vegetables are classified into different types. Those introduced to you here and on pages 76 and 77 are listed according to these types.

Stalk Vegetables

• Artichokes, the thistle vegetable, can be round and pointed, from bright green to violet, fat, slender, large, or tiny. They are obtainable all year-round, but are most readily available in the spring. They keep in the vegetable section of the refrigerator for about 4 days.

• Celery grows in bunches and is available year-round; can be stored for about 2 weeks in the vegetable drawer of the refrigerator.

Leaf Vegetables

• Endive, a typical winter vegetable, is in the stores from October to April. Look for closed sprouts, and don't buy any with green tips. Endive tastes best when you eat it the same day, but stored in the dark in the refrigerator, it will keep for a few days.

• Chard, a member of the beet family, is best used as soon as possible after purchase, but can be stored, wrapped in a plastic bag in the refrigerator, for up to 3 days. Chard has tender greens and crisp stalks. The greens can be prepared like spinach, the stalks like asparagus.

• Spinach can be bought all year-round. Choose leaves that are crisp and dark green with a nice fresh fragrance, and avoid those that are limp, damaged, or that have yellow spots. It tastes good raw or cooked but should not, if possible, be reheated, since this allows its toxic nitrates to develop. It keeps for only a very short time in the vegetable bin of the refrigerator and should be used as soon as possible.

Mushrooms

These delectable fungi are grown in great quantity and are available fresh all year long. Although sizes and shapes vary tremendously and colors can range from white to black with a full gamut of colors in between, the white and brown varieties are the most widely distributed of the various kinds of mushrooms. They can be kept for about 3 days in the vegetable bin of the refrigerator.

Legumes

• **Peas** are harvested from June to the end of September. Sweet sugar snap peas, which have edible pods, are in season from December to September. You should use fresh peas right away.

• You can buy **green beans** year-round. Wrapped in plastic and stored in the vegetable bin of the refrigerator, fresh green beans can be kept for up to 2 days.

The Onion Family

• Fresh **garlic** can be bought any time of year. As a rule, its primary season is the spring and summer, but it is available dried all year-round. Fresh heads are best kept in the vegetable bin of the refrigerator; dried garlic must be stored in a place that is cool, airy, and dry.

• **Leeks** can be kept in the vegetable bin of the refrigerator for a week without any concern. However, it is better to wrap them so that their odor does not spread.

• There are various members of the **onion** family: common yellow onions, Spanish onions, white and red onions, shallots, boiling onions, and scallions are the most important. Scallions are best kept in the refrigerator; the others can be stored for several months in a cool, airy, dry, and dark place. Red onions have the shortest keeping time.

Classic Vegetable Stock—Basic Recipe for about 1¾ quarts (1.75 l)

Wash, pat dry, trim, and chop 2 zucchini; 1 fennel bulb; 2 leeks; 2 stalks celery; 1 bunch each parsley, tarragon, thyme, and basil; 3 onions; 2 cloves garlic. Sauté onions and herbs in 2 tablespoons vegetable oil until aromatic. Add 10 crushed black peppercorns to the rest of the vegetables and garlic in a stockpot and cook over low heat for about 12 minutes, stirring occasionally. Add 2 quarts (2 l) of water, sprinkle in 1 teaspoon salt, and bring to boil. Skim the foam as it rises to the top and let the stock simmer for about 30 minutes. Then strain through fine cheesecloth. The stock will keep in the refrigerator for up to five days. You can, of course, freeze the stock— preferably in small portions corresponding to your needs.

Vegetable Casserole

9 oz (250 g) baking potatoes

salt

9 oz (250 g) green beans

9 oz (250 g) eggplant

9 oz (250 g) zucchini

1¾ lb (750 g) tomatoes

1 large onion

5 tablespoons olive oil

½ bunch each parsley, thyme, and oregano

5 cloves garlic

20 black olives

4½ fl oz (125 mL) vegetable broth

Preparation time: about 2 hours (of which 1¼ hours is cooking time)

Brussels Sprouts en Casserole

18 oz (500 g) baking potatoes

salt

1½ lb (700 g) Brussels sprouts

4 tomatoes

2 garlic cloves

2 sprigs each oregano, thyme, and basil

12 black olives

1 pinch chili powder

1 tablespoon capers

3 tablespoons olive oil

10 oz (300 g) mozzarella

1½ oz (40 g) Parmesan cheese, freshly grated

1 tablespoon butter

oil for casserole

Preparation time: about 50 minutes

Vegetable Casserole

Takes some time • For company

• Wash, peel, slice, and cook potatoes in salted water for about 20 minutes. Trim beans, wash, and halve them crosswise. Cook in boiling salted water for about 7 minutes. Pour off boiling water and stop the cooking with cold water. Wash eggplant, zucchini, and tomatoes, pat dry, and slice about ¼ inch (6 cm) thick. Peel onion and chop coarsely.

• Preheat oven to 350°F (180°C). Butter a baking dish. Layer half the vegetables in dish, season with salt, and drizzle with olive oil.

• Wash the herbs, shake them dry, and chop. Peel and mince garlic. Pit and chop olives. Mix all with the vegetable broth and pour half into baking dish.

• Layer remaining vegetables on top. Pour remaining herb mixture and olive oil over them. Cover with aluminum foil and bake (convection 320°F [160°C]) for about 1¼ hours, removing the foil after 45 minutes. Makes 4 servings.

PER SERVING:	258 CALORIES	
NUTRITIONAL INFORMATION		
Fat (49% calories from fat) 14		g
Protein 7		g
Carbohydrate 26		g
Cholesterol 0		mg
Sodium 416		mg

Brussels Sprouts en Casserole

Pictured • Delicacy from northern Italy

• Wash, peel, and cut potatoes into thin slices. Cook in salted water for about 15 minutes.

• Meanwhile, wash and trim Brussels sprouts, and cut crosses into the stem bases. Steam over boiling water for about 10 minutes. Preheat the oven to 400°F (200°C).

• Wash tomatoes and chop them coarsely, trimming stem bases. Peel and mince garlic. Wash and chop herbs; pit and chop olives.

• Lightly oil a large casserole dish. Lay in potatoes, make a layer of Brussels sprouts on top, and then distribute the tomatoes on top of that. Mix chili powder, olives, capers, garlic, and herbs, sprinkle mixture over vegetables, and drizzle with olive oil. Slice the mozzarella, lay slices over vegetables, and sprinkle with Parmesan. Dot with butter. Bake the casserole (convection 350°F [180°C]) for about 15 minutes. Makes 4 servings.

PER SERVING:	486 CALORIES	
NUTRITIONAL INFORMATION		
Fat (46% calories from fat) 26		g
Protein 28		g
Carbohydrate 41		g
Cholesterol 13		mg
Sodium 195		mg

Moussaka

A Greek classic • Children love it

• Preheat the oven to 350°F (180°C). Wash the potatoes, cover with water, and cook in their skins for 20 to 25 minutes. Then drain the potatoes, peel, and mash them.

• Meanwhile, wash the eggplants, dry them, and cut them into slices about ¼ inch (6 mm) thick. Brush a large baking sheet with 2 tablespoons olive oil, arrange the eggplant slices on it, lightly salt them, drizzle 3 tablespoons olive oil over them, and bake them (convection 320°F [160°C]) for about 20 minutes, turning once after about 10 minutes. Then turn off the oven.

• Meanwhile, peel and finely chop the onions and garlic. Blanch the tomatoes, peel, and dice them, trimming the stem bases. Heat the remaining olive oil in a skillet and sauté the onions and garlic for about 5 minutes or until transparent, then brown them lightly over higher heat. Add the cinnamon and briefly heat it. Add the tomatoes, oregano, salt, pepper, and honey and simmer about 30 minutes, stirring every now and again.

• Meanwhile, roast the pine nuts in a nonstick pan for about 5 minutes until golden brown, stirring constantly. Melt the butter.

• Separate the egg and mix the egg yolk into the mashed potatoes with 1 tablespoon butter, nutmeg, salt, and pepper. Beat the egg white stiff and fold it in.

• Grease a baking dish. Cover the bottom with a layer of eggplant, sprinkle a quarter of the pine nuts on top, and spoon some tomato sauce over. Repeat the procedure twice, then spread the potato on top and sprinkle with the remaining pine nuts. Drizzle the remaining butter over the top. Bake for about 45 minutes. Makes 4 servings.

14 oz (400 g) potatoes
generous 2 lbs (1 kg) eggplant
8 tablespoons olive oil
salt
18 oz (500 g) onions
8 cloves garlic
generous 2 lbs (1 kg) tomatoes
1 generous pinch cinnamon
½ teaspoon oregano
pepper
1 tsp honey
5⅓ oz (150 g) pine nuts
2½ tablespoons butter
1 egg
freshly grated nutmeg
olive oil for the baking dish

Preparation time: about 2 hours (of which 45 minutes is baking time)

PER SERVING:	686 CALORIES	
NUTRITIONAL INFORMATION		
Fat (60% calories from fat) 46	g	
Protein 18	g	
Carbohydrate 51	g	
Cholesterol .170	mg	
Sodium 26	mg	

Broccoli-Potato Casserole

18 oz (500 g) baking potatoes

18 oz (500 g) broccoli

salt

pepper

freshly grated nutmeg

3 tablespoons (50 g) cream

2¾ oz (80 g) Gruyère cheese, freshly grated

1 tablespoon butter

butter for the baking dish

Preparation time: about 50 minutes

Zucchini-Tomato Casserole

18 oz (500 g) zucchini

10 oz (300 g) tomatoes

2 sprigs each basil, oregano, and thyme

½ bunch parsley

10 black olives

2 cloves garlic

7 oz (200 g) feta cheese

salt

pepper

4 tablespoons olive oil

olive oil for the baking dish

Preparation time: about 35 minutes

Broccoli-Potato Casserole

A side dish • Easy to make

• Wash and peel the potatoes, slice them thin, and boil in water to cover for about 15 minutes. Trim the broccoli, wash, and cut it into florets. Place it in a steamer or sieve and steam, covered, over boiling water for about 10 minutes. Preheat the oven to 400°F (200°C).

• Grease a large, shallow baking dish. Make several alternating layers of potatoes and broccoli, lightly salting each layer and seasoning with pepper and nutmeg. Drizzle the cream over the vegetables. Distribute the cheese and butter over the top. Bake the gratin in the oven (convection 350°F [180°C]) for about 15 minutes. Makes 4 servings.

Variation:

Break up 1 can of tuna with a fork and add to the potatoes.

PER SERVING:	254 CALORIES	
NUTRITIONAL INFORMATION		
Fat (47% calories from fat) 14	g
Protein 12	g
Carbohydrate 23	g
Cholesterol .21	mg
Sodium 34	mg

Zucchini-Tomato Casserole

Very easy • Pictured

• Preheat the oven to 400°F (200°C). Brush a large, shallow casserole with olive oil. Wash and dry the zucchini and tomatoes, and cut into thin slices, removing the stem bases. Wash the herbs, shake them dry, and chop. Pit and finely chop the olives. Peel and slice the garlic. Crumble the feta cheese.

• Alternate the zucchini and tomato slices in the casserole, overlapping them. Sprinkle with salt and pepper. Scatter the garlic, herbs, and olives over the top and distribute the olive oil and cheese over all. Bake (convection, 350°F [180°C]) for about 20 minutes. Makes 4 servings.

PER SERVING:	237 CALORIES	
NUTRITIONAL INFORMATION		
Fat (66% calories from fat) 18	g
Protein 12	g
Carbohydrate 10	g
Cholesterol .19	mg
Sodium 108	mg

Chard Casserole

For company • Subtly complex

• Wash the potatoes, peel, and slice them. Boil in salted water to cover for about 15 minutes, then drain.

• Meanwhile, preheat the oven to 350°F (180°C). Trim the chard, wash, and pat it dry. Trim off the coarse stems and cut them into fine strips. Peel and mince the onion and garlic. Wash the herbs, shake them dry, and chop them. Heat 1 tablespoon olive oil in a small pan and sauté the onion and half the garlic for about 3 minutes, stirring. Add the chard stems, salt, thyme, and pepper and cook, stirring, for about 2 minutes.

• Bring plenty of salted water to boil and blanch the chard leaves in it for about 1 minute.

• Wash the tomatoes and dice them, discarding the stem bases. Mix with the remaining garlic and basil and season to taste with salt and pepper. Trim the mushrooms, wipe them clean, and slice them.

• Brush a large, shallow baking dish with olive oil. Cover the bottom with half the chard leaves, lay the potato slices on them very close together, and sprinkle with a third of the Parmesan. Distribute the mushrooms and parsley on top, salt lightly, and sprinkle with another third of the Parmesan. Spread the tomato mixture evenly on top and finish with the remaining chard leaves. Sprinkle with the remaining Parmesan and drizzle with the remaining olive oil. Bake for about 25 minutes (convection 320°F [160°C]). Makes 4 servings.

Variation:

This casserole tastes very good with fish (such as flounder or red snapper fillets). Sprinkle the fish with lemon juice, season with salt and pepper, and cook in 2 to 3 tablespoons butter for about 1 minute on each side. Place the fillets under the last layer of chard leaves. Sprinkling 1 tablespoon pine nuts over the top is a nice finishing touch.

PER SERVING:	285 CALORIES
NUTRITIONAL INFORMATION	
Fat (41% calories from fat) 14	g
Protein 17	g
Carbohydrate 28	g
Cholesterol .13	mg
Sodium 751	mg

14 oz (400 g) baking potatoes
salt
18 oz (500 g) chard
1 onion
6 cloves garlic
1 sprig thyme
½ bunch basil
3 tablespoons olive oil
pepper
14 oz (400 g) tomatoes
10 oz (300 g) mushrooms
3½ oz (100 g) Parmesan, freshly grated
1 bunch parsley
olive oil for the baking dish

Preparation time: about 1 hour

Polenta Casserole with Vegetables

Pictured • Children love it

• Preheat oven to 400°F (200°C). Wash and dry pepper, remove seeds and membranes, and dice. Trim scallions, wash, and slice into rings. Heat 2 tablespoons oil in a skillet and sauté diced pepper for about 2 minutes. Add scallions and oregano and sauté briefly. Add drained corn. Season with salt.

• Bring vegetable stock to boil and vigorously stir in polenta. Remove from heat and let stand, covered, for about 5 minutes. Stir in 2 oz (60 g) cheese. Oil a baking dish well. Spread in half the polenta mixture.

• Fold eggs and 2 oz (60 g) cheese into vegetables. Season to taste with cayenne and spread over the polenta in the dish. Top with remaining polenta.

• Melt the butter and brush it onto the polenta. Sprinkle with rest of cheese and bake (convection 350°F [180°C]) about 35 minutes. Makes 4 servings.

PER SERVING:	503 CALORIES	
NUTRITIONAL INFORMATION		
Fat (47% calories from fat) 26	g
Protein 22	g
Carbohydrate 45	g
Cholesterol .201	mg
Sodium 1891	mg

Endive Casserole

Classic • Easy to make

• Peel the potatoes, slice, and simmer in salted water for about 15 minutes. Drain. Bring water to boil in two pots. Trim the endive, wash, and cut it into strips. Wash the carrots, peel, and slice diagonally. Cook the endive and carrot separately for about 5 minutes.

• Meanwhile, clean the scallions and slice them into rings. Heat the olive oil and sauté the scallions for about 3 minutes. Wash the parsley, shake it dry, and chop.

• Butter a casserole dish well. Lay the potatoes in it and put the carrots on top. Sprinkle the scallions on top of that and distribute the endive over all. Season with pepper.

• Beat the eggs and stir in the cheese and cornstarch. Fold in the parsley and distribute the mixture over the endive. Sprinkle the sunflower seeds over the top and bake for about 25 minutes in the oven (convection 320°F [160°C]). Makes 4 servings.

PER SERVING:	310 CALORIES	
NUTRITIONAL INFORMATION		
Fat (45% calories from fat) 16	g
Protein 15	g
Carbohydrate 29	g
Cholesterol .222	mg
Sodium 58	mg

Polenta Casserole

1 red bell pepper
2 scallions
3 tablespoons vegetable oil
1 teaspoon dried oregano
1 can corn (14 oz [400 g])
salt
2 cups (16 fl oz/500 ml) vegetable stock (page 59) or broth
1 cup (3½ oz/100 g) polenta
5 oz (150 g) Emmentaler, freshly grated
2 eggs
cayenne pepper
2 tablespoons butter
oil for the baking dish

*Preparation time:
about 1 hour*

Endive Casserole

18 oz (500 g) potatoes
salt
1 medium head endive (about 26 oz [750 g])
9 oz. (250 g) carrots
4 scallions
3 tablespoons olive oil
1 bunch parsley
black pepper
2 eggs
10 oz (300 g) ricotta or small-curd cottage cheese
2 tablespoons cornstarch
2 tablespoons sunflower seeds
melted butter for the baking dish

*Preparation time:
about 1 hour*

Kohlrabi-Carrot Casserole

salt
14 oz (400 g) kohlrabi
14 oz (400 g) carrots
2 eggs
1 generous cup (9 fl oz/250 ml) cream
freshly grated nutmeg
grated peel of ½ orange
1 tablespoon cornstarch
3 tablespoons orange juice
1 tablespoon coarsely chopped hazelnuts
butter for the baking dish

Preparation time: about 45 minutes

Spinach Lasagne

10 oz (300 g) mushrooms
1 onion
1 clove garlic
4 tablespoons butter
14 oz (400 g) fresh spinach
1 cup (8 oz/250 ml) vegetable broth
1½ tablespoons all-purpose flour
1 cup (8 fl oz/250 ml) milk
salt
freshly grated nutmeg
8 uncooked lasagne noodles
3½ oz (100 g) Parmesan, freshly grated
butter for the baking dish

Preparation time: about 1 hour

Kohlrabi-Carrot Casserole

Pictured • Subtle

• Preheat the oven to 400°F (200°C). Bring two pots of salted water to boil. Wash, trim, peel, and thinly slice the kohlrabi and carrots. Blanch each separately for about 4 minutes. Drain.

• Separate the eggs. Whisk the egg yolks and cream together, season with nutmeg, and add the orange peel. Mix the cornstarch and the orange juice and stir in. Beat the egg whites stiff with a pinch of salt and fold into the yolk mixture.

• Grease a casserole dish and arrange a layer of kohlrabi slices in it. Add a layer of carrots and some of the egg mixture. Make several more layers, depending on the size of the casserole. Finish with egg mixture. Sprinkle the hazelnuts over the top and bake (convection 350°F [180°C]) for about 20 minutes. Makes 4 servings.

PER SERVING:	260 CALORIES	
NUTRITIONAL INFORMATION		
Fat (53% calories from fat)	16	g
Protein	10	g
Carbohydrate	21	g
Cholesterol	333	mg
Sodium	43	mg

Spinach Lasagne

For company • Inexpensive

• Preheat oven to 400°F (200°C). Trim mushrooms, wipe clean, and slice them paper thin. Peel and mince onion and garlic. Heat 2 tablespoons butter and sauté mushrooms and onion in it for about 4 minutes.

• Pick over the spinach, wash it, and let it wilt in boiling vegetable broth. Press out liquid and chop spinach. Cook briefly with 1 tablespoon butter and garlic.

• To make white sauce, heat remaining butter and brown the flour in it. Heat milk and whisk into flour mixture. Bring to boil and season with salt and nutmeg.

• Grease a baking dish. Lay two lasagne noodles in it and spread a third of the spinach and broth over them. Put a third of the mushrooms and the white sauce over the top. Repeat twice more, finishing with lasagne noodles. Pour remaining sauce on top and sprinkle with Parmesan. Bake (convection 350°F [180°C]) for about 15 minutes. Makes 4 servings.

PER SERVING:	472 CALORIES	
NUTRITIONAL INFORMATION		
Fat (41% calories from fat)	19	g
Protein	20	g
Carbohydrate	43	g
Cholesterol	46	mg
Sodium	64	mg

14 oz (400 g) tomatoes

5 oz (150 g) each carrots, zucchini, green beans, scallions, and peas

2 tablespoons olive oil

3 tablespoons butter

½ teaspoon dried thyme

salt

pepper

1½ tablespoons all-purpose flour

1 cup (8 oz/250 ml) milk

freshly grated nutmeg

1 tablespoon chopped fresh parsley

8 uncooked lasagne noodles

7 oz (200 g) Parmesan, freshly grated

oil for the baking dish

Preparation time: about 1½ hours (of which 40 minutes is baking time)

Vegetable Lasagne

Needs some time • Can be prepared ahead of time

• Wash and trim all the vegetables. Cut out the stem bases of the tomatoes. Blanch them, cut in half horizontally, remove the seeds, and cut the tomatoes into pieces.

• Peel the carrots and chop fine with the zucchini, beans, and scallions.

• Preheat the oven to 400°F (200°C). Heat the olive oil and 2 tablespoons butter and cook the vegetables with the peas and thyme over medium heat for about 10 minutes. Add the diced tomatoes and cook together for about 5 more minutes. Season with salt and pepper.

• To make white sauce, heat the remaining butter in a small saucepan. Brown the flour in it. Heat the milk and whisk into the flour mixture. Bring the sauce to boil and season with salt and nutmeg.

• Stir two-thirds of the sauce into the vegetables. Wash the parsley, shake it dry, chop, and mix it in.

• Oil a baking dish. Make alternating layers of pasta and vegetables in it, starting with the lasagne and finishing with vegetables. Distribute the remaining sauce on top and sprinkle with cheese. Bake (convection 350°F [180°C]) for about 40 minutes. Makes 4 servings.

Variation:

This dish is also very good made with eggplant and zucchini. Wash 14 oz (400 g) each of eggplant and zucchini, dry, trim, and cut them into lengthwise slices. Fry on both sides, one after the other in 3 tablespoons olive oil each. Season with salt and pepper. Layer as described above, but put some sauce on each layer of eggplant and zucchini. Shorten the baking time to about 30 minutes.

PER SERVING:	639 CALORIES
NUTRITIONAL INFORMATION	

Fat (47% calories from fat) 30	g
Protein 32	g
Carbohydrate 47	g
Cholesterol 60	mg
Sodium 13	mg

The
Art of
packaging

Rolled and Filled

Vegetables, cheese, rice, and nuts can be attractively packaged in endive, chard, or cabbage, or rolled in crepes. All large-leaved vegetables are suitable for the purpose. These and their other "colleagues" are presented on the following pages and on pages 58 and 59.

Fruit Vegetables

• **Eggplant** is available year-round. Since it is a delicate vegetable, it should not be kept in the refrigerator for longer than 2 days and shouldn't be stored with tomatoes or fruit.

• **Peppers** come in various types, shapes, colors, and stages of ripeness. Though at their peak in the summer, they are available year-round. They keep in the vegetable bin of the refrigerator for up to 10 days.

• **Field-grown tomatoes** are available in the summertime; those grown under glass can be bought all year. Kept in the refrigerator, tomatoes lose their flavor. Let hard tomatoes ripen at room temperature; ripe tomatoes keep fresh for about 3 days.

• **Zucchini** are available all year long but are especially abundant in summer and fall. They keep in the vegetable drawer of the refrigerator for up to 2 weeks.

Roots and Tubers

• **Potatoes** are classified into firm-cooking, predominantly firm-cooking, and baking varieties. Always remove green spots and sprouts. You can store potatoes in a cool, dry, and dark place for up to several months, depending on the variety—but never in the refrigerator!

• **Celery root** (celeriac) is most readily available from September through May. It keeps fresh for about 3 weeks in the vegetable bin of the refrigerator.

• **Carrots** are available year-round. They keep in the refrigerator for a week or more. Always cut off the greens of bunched carrots before storing them because they draw off moisture.

Cabbage Family

• **Cauliflower** comes in three basic colors: white (the most popular and readily available), green, and purple (a vibrant violet that turns pale green when cooked). Cauliflower is composed of bunches of tiny florets on clusters of stalks. The entire floret is edible. Refrigerate raw cauliflower, tightly wrapped, for 3 to 5 days; cooked for 1 to 3 days.

• **Broccoli** should be firm, tight-budded, and bluish-green when you buy it. It keeps in the refrigerator for up to 4 days, if placed unwashed in an airtight bag; otherwise, it keeps in the refrigerator for about 2 days.

• **Cabbage** is a typical winter vegetable, though it is available all year-round. Cabbage comes in many forms—the shapes can be flat, conical, or round; the heads compact or loose; and the leaves curly or plain. Choose a cabbage with fresh, crisp-looking leaves that are firmly packed; the head should be heavy for its size. The heads keep for about 1 week in the vegetable bin of the refrigerator.

• **Kohlrabi** is in season from April to October. Both the purple-tinged, white bulblike stem and the greens of the kohlrabi are edible. The kohlrabi bulb tastes like a mild, sweet turnip. Choose a kohlrabi that is heavy for its size with firm, deeply colored green leaves. You can safely keep it in the vegetable bin of the refrigerator for 1 week, but always cut off the leaflets first.

• **Brussels sprouts**, members of the cabbage family that resemble tiny cabbage heads, are in season from the end of August until December. Buy small bright green sprouts with compact heads. They only keep for about 2 days in the refrigerator.

• **Endive** is available all year. There are three basic varieties of endive: Belgian endive (also known as French endive and witloof or white leaf), curly endive, and escarole. Depending on the variety of endive, it can keep for from 1 to about 3 days in the vegetable bin of the refrigerator.

Extra-Hearty Vegetable Stock (Basic Recipe for 2 quart [2 l])

Trim, wash, and dice 3 large carrots, 2 leeks, 3 stalks celery, 1 celery root, 4 tomatoes, 3½ oz (100 g) mushrooms, 2 onions, and 6 cloves garlic. Chop 2 bunches parsley and 3 sprigs each thyme and marjoram. Heat 2 tablespoons vegetable oil in a stockpot. Fry the onions and herbs in it until aromatic. Coarsely crush 10 peppercorns and add with 2 bay leaves, the vegetables, and the garlic. Cook all together over low heat for about 12 minutes, stirring occasionally. Pour in 2½ quarts (2.5 l) water, add salt, and bring to boil. Skim the foam that rises to the top and let the stock simmer for about 1½ hours. Finally, strain through fine cheesecloth. The stock will keep in the refrigerator for up to five days; freeze it for longer storage. You will find a classic stock on page 59.

77

salt

1 small red cabbage (about 2¼ lb/1 kg)

3½ oz (100 g) mushrooms

1 onion

3 cloves garlic

4 tablespoons vegetable oil

3 tablespoons butter

3½ oz (100 g) whole-wheat bread crumbs

6 oz (175 g) mixed nuts (Brazil nuts, cashews, walnuts, hazelnuts), chopped

1 tablespoon herbes de Provence

grated peel of 1 lemon

pepper

1¼ cups (10 fl oz/300 ml) vegetable stock (page 77) or broth

Scant ½ cup (3½ oz/100 g) plain yogurt

⅔ cup (5⅓ oz/150 g) sour cream or crème fraîche

½ teaspoon sweet paprika

Preparation time: about 1¼ hours (of which 45 minutes is baking time)

Red Cabbage Roll with Nut Filling

Subtle • Somewhat time-consuming

• Bring plenty of salted water to boil in a large pot. Core the cabbage with a wedge-shaped cut. Cook the cabbage in the salted water for about 15 minutes. Take it out and carefully loosen 8 to 12 outer leaves, lay them on a dish towel, and pat them dry. Plane the central ribs flat with a sharp knife. Cut the rest of the cabbage into fine strips.

• Preheat the oven to 350°F (180°C). For the filling, trim the mushrooms, wipe them clean, and chop them fine. Peel and finely chop the onion and garlic. Heat 1 teaspoon oil and ½ tablespoon butter in a skillet and fry the bread crumbs and nuts in it for about 3 minutes. Transfer the mixture to a bowl. Wipe out the skillet. Heat the remaining oil and 1 tablespoon butter in the skillet and sauté the onion until transparent. Add the mushrooms and cabbage strips and braise over medium heat, without browning, for about 5 minutes. Stir in the garlic and herbs and continue cooking for 2 minutes. Add to the nut mixture.

• Mix half the lemon peel with salt, pepper, and the vegetable stock.

• Grease an 11-inch (28-cm) baking dish. Spread out the cabbage leaves so that the walls and bottom of the dish are completely covered and the leaves are standing up over the edges. Reserve some cabbage leaves for covering.

• Spread the filling in the center of the baking dish and dot with the remaining butter. Lay the remaining cabbage leaves on top and fold the upright leaf edges down over them. Pour the vegetable stock mixture over the cabbage leaves. Cover with aluminum foil and bake (convection 320°F [160°C]) for about 45 minutes.

• For the sauce, mix the yogurt, sour cream, paprika, salt, and remaining lemon peel. Slice the red cabbage roll and serve with the sauce. Makes 4 servings.

PER SERVING:	712 CALORIES	
NUTRITIONAL INFORMATION		
Fat (69% calories from fat) 55		g
Protein 15		g
Carbohydrate 42		g
Cholesterol 55		mg
Sodium 546		mg

Chinese Cabbage Rolls

Easy to make • Subtle

• Cut the tofu into small cubes. Peel and grate the ginger. Peel and mince the garlic. Combine the soy sauce, ginger, chili pepper, and garlic and marinate the tofu cubes in the mixture for about 1 hour. Drain the tofu, reserving the marinade.

• Bring a large pot of salted water to boil. Core the cabbage and cook it in the boiling salted water for about 15 minutes. Preheat the oven to 350°F (180°C).

• Remove the cabbage and drain it. Carefully remove 12 outer leaves, lay them on a dish towel, and press them dry. Plane the center ribs flat with a sharp knife. Cut the remaining cabbage into thin strips. Wash the carrots and celery. Peel the carrots and the thick outer strings of the celery, if necessary. Trim the scallions, wash them, and slice into thin rings. Wash the bean sprouts and drain well.

• In a small skillet heat ½ tablespoon of oil and fry ½ tablespoon sesame seeds and the tofu cubes, until the seeds are golden. Pour in the marinade

and simmer gently until slightly thickened. Mix in the sliced cabbage, carrots, celery, scallions, sprouts, and salt to taste.

• Place 2 tablespoons filling on each cabbage leaf. Fold over the cabbage leaves, roll them up, and fasten with 2 toothpicks apiece.

• Heat the remaining oil in a shallow, flameproof baking dish. Arrange the cabbage rolls tightly in the dish and sear briefly until they are golden brown on the bottom. Sprinkle with the remaining sesame seeds.

• Pour the vegetable broth over them to a depth of about ¼ inch (1 cm). Bring to boil on top of the stove, then bake the cabbage rolls (convection 320°F [160°C]) for about 20 minutes, basting occasionally and adding more broth if necessary. Serve with Thai chili sauce. Makes 4 servings.

PER SERVING:	205 CALORIES
NUTRITIONAL INFORMATION	

Fat (41% calories from fat) 10	g
Protein 10	g
Carbohydrate 22	g
Cholesterol 1	mg
Sodium 1525	mg

3½ oz (100 g) tofu

1½-inch (2-cm) piece fresh ginger

2 cloves garlic

4 tablespoons soy sauce

pinch of chili pepper

salt

1 small head white cabbage (about 2¼ lb/1 kg)

3 to 4 oz (100 g) carrots

2 oz (50 g) celery

3 scallions

3 to 4 oz (100 g) bean sprouts

2½ tablespoons oil

1 tablespoon sesame seeds

1 cup (8 fl oz/250 ml) vegetable broth

24 toothpicks for fastening

purchased sweet-and-sour Thai chili sauce

oil for the baking dish

Preparation time: about 1¼ hours

Crepe Packets with Two Fillings
Somewhat time-consuming • For company

• For the batter, sift the flour into a bowl. Beat the milk and eggs together and stir into the flour. Season with salt and let the batter rest for 1 hour. Then melt the butter and stir it in.

• Melt some clarified butter in a crepe pan. Add 3 to 4 tablespoons of batter and tilt the pan to distribute the batter evenly across the entire bottom. As soon as the batter is firm, turn the crepe with a spatula. Make 8 crepes in this manner and keep them warm. Preheat the oven to 400°F (200°C). Grease 4 individual gratin dishes.

• For the Roquefort filling, peel the apples and dice them, discarding the core and seeds. Pour the sherry over them. Crumble the Roquefort, chop the walnuts, and mix both with the apples. Divide the filling among 4 crepes. Fold up the crepes like an envelope and place one in each gratin dish.

• For the mushroom filling, trim the mushrooms, wipe them clean, and chop them. Peel and mince the shallots. Heat the butter in a skillet and fry the mushrooms and shallots for about 4 minutes, seasoning them with salt and pepper. Deglaze with wine and cook over moderate heat until the liquid has evaporated. Let cool somewhat and fold in the Gouda. Distribute this filling among the other 4 crepes, fold each one up like an envelope, and place beside the other crepes.

• Mix the pecorino with the hazelnuts and scatter it over the crepes. Bake (convection 350°F [180°C]) for about 15 minutes. Makes 4 servings.

Tip

Since the crepe batter should rest for at least 1 hour before you cook it, it's wise to make the crepes the day before when you are planning this dish for company. Wrapped in plastic, they keep for about 3 days in the refrigerator. You can also fill the crepes with fruit and cottage cheese, frozen yogurt, or ice cream and have them for dessert. There are no limits on your imagination.

PER SERVING:	776 CALORIES	
NUTRITIONAL INFORMATION		
Fat (58% calories from fat) 46	g
Protein 33	g
Carbohydrate 44	g
Cholesterol .377	mg
Sodium 342	mg

For the crepes:
1⅓ cups (5⅓ oz/150 g) all-purpose flour
1 cup (8 fl oz/250 ml) milk
2 eggs
salt
1½ tablespoons butter

For the Roquefort filling:
2 small apples
2 tablespoons sherry (or orange juice)
3 oz (75 g) Roquefort cheese
2 oz (50 g) walnuts

For the mushroom filling:
3 to 4 oz (100 g) mushrooms
2 shallots
2 tablespoons butter
pepper
salt
3 tablespoons white wine (or vegetable broth)
3 oz (75 g) Gouda cheese, freshly grated

For the topping:
3½ oz (100 g) pecorino cheese, freshly grated
2 oz (50 g) hazelnuts
clarified butter for frying and for the baking dish

Resting time: 1 hour

Preparation time: about 1 hour

83

Pancake Rolls

2 eggs • 6 egg yolks

2¼ cups (18 fl oz/550 ml) milk

1⅓ cups (5⅓ oz/150 g) all-purpose flour

salt

3 tablespoons clarified butter

7 oz (200 g) fresh spinach leaves

3½ oz (100 g) walnuts

4 tablespoons walnut oil

7 oz (200 g) low-fat cottage cheese

freshly grated nutmeg

4 to 5 oz (125 g) mozzarella cheese

Resting time: 1 hour

Preparation time: about 1½ hours

Endive Packets

1 red and 1 yellow pepper

1 small head curly endive

salt

4½ tablespoons olive oil

3 to 4 oz (100 g) feta cheese

pepper

½ bunch marjoram

½ bunch parsley

2 cloves garlic

6 black olives

1¾ oz (50 g) whole-wheat bread crumbs

1 teaspoon chopped fresh rosemary

grated peel of 1 lemon

Preparation time: about 50 minutes

Pancake Rolls

Subtle • Pictured

• Beat 2 eggs, 1 egg yolk, 1 cup (8 fl oz/ 250 ml) milk, flour, and salt together. Let the batter rest for about 1 hour. Then cook 10 to 12 pancakes in a skillet in hot clarified butter.

• Preheat oven to 350°F (180°C). Bring a little salted water to boil in a large pot. Pick over the spinach, wash, and let wilt in the boiling water. Drain, press out as much moisture as possible, and chop. Finely chop half the walnuts; coarsely chop the remainder.

• Whisk 4 egg yolks until smooth with oil and cottage cheese. Mix in spinach and finely chopped nuts and season to taste with nutmeg and salt.

• Grease a baking dish. Spread the pancakes with spinach mixture, roll up, and arrange in baking dish. Dice the mozzarella and distribute over the top, along with coarsely chopped nuts. Beat remaining egg yolk with the remaining 1¼ cups (10 fl oz/300 ml) milk and pour it over the top. Bake (convection 320°F [160°C]) for about 45 minutes. Makes 4 servings.

PER SERVING:	915 CALORIES	
NUTRITIONAL INFORMATION		
Fat (59% calories from fat) 53	g
Protein 45	g
Carbohydrate 37	g
Cholesterol 1086	mg
Sodium 28	mg

Endive Packets

Easy to make • Inexpensive

• Broil the peppers for about 12 minutes or until the skins blister, turning once. Transfer peppers to plastic bag and let cool. Set oven at 400°F (200°C). Skin peppers, halve, and trim out seeds and white membranes.

• Meanwhile, trim endive, wash it, and remove eight leaves. Blanch in boiling water for about 8 minutes and pat dry. Plane the center ribs flat with a sharp knife. Coat a baking dish with ½ tablespoon olive oil.

• Cut peppers and feta into small cubes, season with salt and pepper, and distribute among endive leaves. Roll up leaves and arrange in baking dish, seam side down.

• Wash herbs, shake them dry, and chop the leaflets. Peel and mince garlic. Pit olives and chop finely. Mix herbs, garlic, and olives with all the remaining ingredients and sprinkle over the packets. Brown in the oven (convection 350°F [180°C]) for about 10 minutes. Makes 4 servings.

PER SERVING:	219 CALORIES	
NUTRITIONAL INFORMATION		
Fat (54% calories from fat) 14	g
Protein 9	g
Carbohydrate 17	g
Cholesterol 10	mg
Sodium 97	mg

Celery Root and Vegetable Strudel

Inexpensive • Children like it

• Separate the phyllo leaves and spread them out on a dampened dish towel.

• For the filling, bring a saucepan of salted water to boil. Wash the celery root, peel, and dice. Cook in the boiling water until tender, about 10 minutes. Drain and puree. Refrigerate the puree for about 30 minutes.

• Preheat the oven to 400°F (200°C). Grease a baking sheet. Dice the tofu and puree with the egg white. Blend the cream, celery root puree, and tofu mixture well. Season with salt, pepper, and nutmeg.

• Wash the leek, zucchini, and carrots, trim, and cut them into thin sticks. Heat the butter and braise the vegetables in it without letting them brown. Season with salt and pepper. Let cool somewhat.

• Spread the celery root mixture on the phyllo, leaving a border about 1½ inches (4 cm) wide. Distribute the vegetables on top of the puree and roll up with the help of the dish towel. Brush the seam edges with egg yolk and press them together. Fold the ends closed and lay the strudel on the baking sheet, seam side down.

• Brush the strudel with the remaining egg yolk. Bake (convection 350°F [180°C]) for about 25 minutes. Meanwhile, for the sauce, wash the vegetables, trim them, and cut them into small cubes. Wash the parsley, shake it dry, and chop. Heat the butter and sauté the vegetables in it for about 3 minutes. Deglaze with the cream, allowing it to simmer briefly. Add the parsley and season to taste with salt and nutmeg. Slice the strudel and serve with the sauce. Makes 4 to 6 servings.

Variation:

Rub 7 oz (200 g) halibut or fillet of sole with lemon, salt, and pepper, and cut into strips. Cook in 2 tablespoons butter just until opaque and distribute over the celery root puree with the vegetables. Then roll up as described above.

PER SERVING:	211 CALORIES
NUTRITIONAL INFORMATION	
Fat (56% calories from fat) 13	g
Protein 4	g
Carbohydrate .19	g
Cholesterol 73	mg
Sodium 41	mg

1 package phyllo dough (5 to 6 leaves required)

For the filling:
salt
7 oz (200 g) celery root
2 oz (50 g) tofu
1 egg white
2 tablespoons cream
white pepper
freshly grated nutmeg
1 leek
1 zucchini
2 carrots
1 tablespoon butter

For the sauce:
½ leek
½ zucchini
1 small carrot
½ bunch parsley
1 tablespoon butter
7 tablespoons cream
salt
freshly grated nutmeg
1 egg yolk
grease for the baking sheet

Preparation time:
about 1 hour and 10 minutes

Mini Eggplant Rolls in Tomato Sauce
Somewhat time consuming • Decorative

For the sauce:
2¼ lb (1 kg) ripe plum tomatoes
4 tablespoons olive oil
1 clove garlic
2 sprigs thyme
salt
pepper

For the filling:
1 bunch each parsley and basil
3 tablespoons olive oil
4 tablespoons bread crumbs
4 tablespoons pecorino cheese, freshly grated
2 garlic cloves
salt
5 oz (150 g) mozzarella cheese

For the mini rolls:
4 long eggplants
wooden skewers
4 tablespoons olive oil for the baking sheet

Preparation time: about 1¼ hours

• For the sauce, blanch the tomatoes, peel, and dice them, discarding the stem bases. Heat the olive oil and simmer the tomatoes in it. Peel the garlic and put it through a press into the tomatoes. Wash the thyme, shake it dry, chop the leaflets, and add them to the sauce. Season with salt and pepper and simmer for about 30 minutes.

• For the filling, wash the herbs, shake them dry, and chop. Heat 1 tablespoon olive oil and brown the bread crumbs in it. Mix with the herbs, cheese, and 2 tablespoons olive oil. Peel the garlic, put through a press, and mix it in. Season with salt and pepper. Cut the mozzarella into thin slices.

• Preheat the oven to 400°F (200°C). For the mini rolls, wash the eggplants, remove the stems and bases, and cut lengthwise into slices about ⅛ inch (3 mm) thick. Spread the herb mixture evenly on the eggplant slices. Cover with mozzarella slices and roll up the eggplant. Fasten with wooden skewers.

• Drizzle olive oil on the baking sheet and turn the eggplant mini rolls in it to coat them. Bake the rolls (convection 350°F [180°C]) for about 15 minutes. Serve with the tomato sauce. Makes 4 servings

Variation:

You can also prepare this dish with zucchini, provided you get large, thick ones that are frequently available in the summer. Since zucchini is blander than eggplant, however, try Gouda or Emmentaler instead of mozzarella; you can grate the cheese coarsely instead of slicing it.

PER SERVING:	444 CALORIES
NUTRITIONAL INFORMATION	
Fat (69% calories from fat) . . . . .34 g	
Protein . . . . .18 g	
Carbohydrate . . . . .16 g	
Cholesterol .7 mg	
Sodium . . . . .22 mg	

Baked Cabbage Rolls

Inexpensive • Takes some time

• Bring a large pot of salted water to boil. Core the cabbage and boil with the caraway seeds for about 20 minutes.

• Meanwhile, cook the rice in 1¼ cups (10 fl oz/300 ml) salted water for about 10 minutes; drain.

• Drain the cabbage and remove 8 outside leaves. Lay them on a dish towel and pat dry. Plane the center ribs flat with a sharp knife. Cut the remaining cabbage into fine strips.

• Peel and finely chop the onions. Cut the stem bases from 2 tomatoes. Blanch and peel the tomatoes, halve them crosswise, remove the seeds, and dice. Coarsely grate the cheese. Mix the onion, tomatoes, cheese, rice, and chopped cabbage and fold in the beaten egg. Season with salt and pepper.

• Half overlap 2 cabbage leaves and distribute the filling on them. Roll the leaves up to make a cylinder. Repeat with the remaining leaves. Oil a baking dish. Heat 4 tablespoons oil in a skillet and braise the cabbage rolls without letting them brown. Arrange them side by side in the baking dish. Coarsely dice the remaining tomato and add to the baking dish with the broth. Mix the bread crumbs, Parmesan, and thyme and distribute over the cabbage rolls. Bake (convection 320°F [160°C]) for about 40 minutes.

• Wash the parsley, shake it dry, and chop. Transfer the cabbage rolls to a platter and keep them warm. Strain the juices and bring them to boil with the tomato puree. Season to taste with salt, pepper, and the sugar and serve with the cabbage rolls. Makes 4 servings.

salt
1 medium head cabbage
1 teaspoon caraway seeds
⅔ cup (5⅓ oz/150 g) long-grain rice
1 large onion
3 meaty tomatoes
3 to 4 oz (100 g) Emmentaler cheese
3 to 4 oz (100 g) Gouda cheese
1 egg
pepper
4 tablespoons oil
½ cup (4 fl oz/125 ml) vegetable broth
4 tablespoons bread crumbs
½ oz (40 g) Parmesan cheese, freshly grated
pinch of dried thyme
1 bunch parsley
1 generous cup (9 oz/250 g) canned tomato puree
pinch of sugar
oil for the baking dish

Preparation time: about 1½ hours (of which 40 minutes is baking time)

PER SERVING:	607 CALORIES
NUTRITIONAL INFORMATION	
Fat (43% calories from fat) 30	g
Protein 29	g
Carbohydrate 61	g
Cholesterol 191	mg
Sodium 423	mg

Pepper Rolls

Pepper Rolls

4 red bell peppers
4 yellow bell peppers
2 cloves garlic
14 oz (400 g) fresh spinach
salt
10 oz (300 g) feta cheese
2 eggs
½ bunch each mint, thyme, and oregano, finely chopped
pepper
2 tablespoons butter
butter for the baking dish
wooden skewers

Preparation time:
about 50 minutes

Chard Packets

1 scant cup (7 oz/200 g) rice
3 cups (24 fl oz/750 ml) vegetable broth
salt
2¼ lb (1 kg) chard
2 carrots
1 onion
1 ¾-inch (2-cm) piece fresh ginger
2 tablespoons butter
2 tablespoons cream
1 egg
½ teaspoon curry powder
8 wooden skewers
butter for the baking dish

Preparation time:
about 50 minutes

Pepper Rolls
Somewhat time consuming • Pictured

• Broil peppers for about 12 minutes or until skins are dark brown and blistered, turning them once. Transfer peppers to a plastic bag and let cool.

• Preheat oven to 350°F (180°C). Peel and force garlic through a press. Bring a small amount of water to boil. Pick over spinach, wash it, and let it wilt in boiling water. Drain and cool, then squeeze out as much moisture as possible. Chop the spinach coarsely and season with salt. In a separate bowl, thoroughly mix feta, eggs, garlic, herbs, and pepper.

• Open up peppers with a lengthwise cut on one side and clean out insides. Carefully pull off skin, leaving each pepper in one piece. Open up each pepper, spread the inside with spinach, then spread feta mixture on top. Roll up and fasten with a wooden skewer.

• Grease a small baking dish and arrange the pepper rolls in it, close together. Dot with butter and bake (convection 320°F [160°C]) for about 20 minutes. Makes 4 servings.

PER SERVING:	375 CALORIES	
NUTRITIONAL INFORMATION		
Fat (56% calories from fat) 24	g
Protein 25	g
Carbohydrate 18	g
Cholesterol 347	mg
Sodium 62	mg

Chard Packets
For company • Subtle

• Cook the rice in 2 cups (16 fl oz/500 ml) vegetable broth until broth is absorbed, about 20 minutes. Bring plenty of salted water to boil in a large pot. Wash and trim chard; cut off and discard the thick stalks. Blanch the leaves for about 2 minutes, then drain. Plane the leaf ribs flat with a sharp knife.

• Peel and mince carrots, onion, and ginger. Sauté in the butter without browning for about 5 minutes. Preheat the oven to 350°F (180°C).

• Mix rice, carrots, onion, and ginger with the cream, egg, and curry powder.

• Lay out chard leaves on a work surface (if they are small, stack two for each roll) and heap filling in the center. Fold in the sides of leaves and roll up.

• Grease a baking dish. Arrange chard packets in it and pour remaining vegetable broth over them. Bake (convection 320°F [160°C]) for about 30 minutes. Makes 4 servings.

PER SERVING:	329 CALORIES	
NUTRITIONAL INFORMATION		
Fat (28% calories from fat) 10	g
Protein 11	g
Carbohydrate 48	g
Cholesterol .96	mg
Sodium 2545	mg

INDEX

Published originally under
the title *Vegetarisches Aus Dem
BACKOFEN*
© 1998 by Gräfe und Unzer
Verlag GmbH, München
English translation © Copyright
2000 by Barron's Educational
Series, Inc.
German edition by Gabriele Redden
Photography by Heinz-Josef Beckers
Cover photo: Michael Brauner
English translation by Elizabeth D.
Crawford

All inquiries should be addressed to:
Barron's Educational Series, Inc.
250 Wireless Boulevard
Hauppauge, NY 11788
http://www.barronseduc.com

Library of Congress Catalog Card
No. 99-86988

International Standard Book No.
0-7641-1279-1

**Library of Congress Cataloging-in-
Publication Data**
Redden, Gabriele.
    [Vegetarisches aus dem
    Backofen. English]
    Oven-baked vegetarian dishes /
Gabriele Redden ; photography,
Heinz-Josef Beckers ; title picture,
Michael Brauner ; translation from
the German, Elizabeth D. Crawford.
        p. cm.
    Includes index.
    ISBN 0-7641-1279-1
    1. Vegetarian cookery. I. Title.

TX837 .R4413 2000
641.5'636–dc21
                                    99-86988

Printed in Hong Kong
9 8 7 6 5 4 3 2 1

Gabriele Redden ran a small
cookbook-publishing house for
4 years, then headed the cooking
department of a well-known
women's magazine for 10 years.
Today she is a freelance journalist
and cookbook author with homes
in Munich and Majorca.

Heinz-Josef Beckers studied
communications design at the
University of Essen (Folkwang) in
Germany. He specializes in food,
still life, and experimental
photography as well as conceptual
and graphic design work for
corporations, publishers, and
advertising agencies.

Cheese for Oven-Baked Dishes

These cheeses are the best choices for fillings and gratins. The fat content always refers to the cheese's dry measure. If you want to know how much fat the cheese actually contains, multiply the percentage given for the particular cheese:

for fresh cheese   by 0.3
for soft cheese   by 0.4
for semihard cheese   by 0.5
for hard cheese   by 0.6

Camembert

Originally from Normandy, Camembert is the most famous soft cheese with a crust of white mold. Formerly it was only produced from the raw milk of cows or goats, but today it is primarily made from pasteurized cow or goat milk. Camembert has a fat content between 30 percent and 70 percent. It ripens in only 9 to 15 days and, depending on the degree of ripeness, has a mild and creamy to piquant flavor.

Emmentaler

Whether from Bavaria or Switzerland, this hard cheese is produced from raw milk, ripens in 3 to 12 months, and has at least 45 percent fat. With its strong, nutty flavor, it is particularly suited for hearty dishes.

Feta

Genuine Greek feta is produced exclusively from sheep's milk. After being formed and pressed, it is kept airtight by immersion in brine. Feta produced in other countries may be made from cow's milk. This fresh cheese has a fat content of at least 45 percent.